A Williamson Multicultural *Kids Can!*® Book

THE KIDS' MULTICULTURAL CRAFT BOOK

35 CRAFTS FROM AROUND THE WORLD

Roberta Gould

**Illustrations by
Sarah Rakitin**

Williamson Publishing W Charlotte, Vermont

Library of Congress Cataloging-in-Publication Data

Gould, Roberta, 1946-
    The kids' multicultural craft book : 35 crafts from around the world / Roberta Gould ; illustrations by Sarah Rakitin.
        p. cm. -- (A Williamson multicultural kids can! book)
Includes index.
Summary: Provides instructions for creating 35 handicraft projects inspired by past and present cultures from around the world. Includes background information on the various crafts.
    ISBN 1-885593-91-0   (pbk.)
    1.   Handicraft--History--Juvenile literature.   [1. Handicraft.] I. Rakitin, Sarah, ill. II. Title. III. Series.
    TT15.G68 2004
    745.5--dc22

                                              2003062146

Kids Can!® series editor: Susan Williamson
Project editor: Vicky Congdon
Interior design and illustrations: Sarah Rakitin
Author photograph: page 4, © Raphael Shevelev/ A Thousand Words, 1997
Photographs: Roberta Gould
Cover design and illustrations: Michael Kline
Printing: Capital City Press

Williamson Publishing Co.
P.O. Box 185
Charlotte, VT 05445
(800) 234-8791

Manufactured in the United States of America

10 9 8 7 6 5 4 3 2 1

DEDICATION

Dedicated to my 21-year-old son, Peter, who is spending a year teaching on a tiny atoll in the middle of the Pacific Ocean.

ACKNOWLEDGMENTS

Thank you to Vicky Congdon for her positive energy and hard work on this book and to Sarah Rakitin for her wonderful illustrations and design.

Thank you to the kids who came over this summer to help me invent ways to make these projects even more wonderful: Allison, Jeff, Graham, Hannah, Bernadette, Ben K., Sean, Ben P., Stephen, and Justin.

Thanks to Mom, Amy, Chuck, Kristin, and Ron for letting me photograph their beautiful examples of multicultural art.

Thank you to all the fabulous kids I've taught (and learned from) for 15 years at Lake School in Richmond and here at my house, Kidtopia, where the art room stuffed with supplies (mostly recycled) spills out to the farm-like backyard.

··· TABLE OF CONTENTS ···

ABOUT THE AUTHOR

Since 1990, Roberta Gould has organized and run an after-school and summer arts and adventure program for kids called "Amusing Muses" in California. She encourages kids to tap into their own creativity and joyful exuberance, creating with what they have on hand and exploring the crafts and traditions of people the world over.

Roberta has traveled extensively on a small budget in Asia, Mexico, and Europe. She has camped throughout Japan, on porches in Nepal, and on rooftops in India. It is on these trips that her love of varied cultures has gained the depth and breadth that she shares in her teaching and writing.

She once sailed in a small sailboat to Alaska, where she swam with seals, rowed among icebergs, ice skated on a glacial lake, climbed up mossy water-falls, and saw a tree filled with eagles. She has kept goats, milked cows, watched her bees swarm, and found her "missing" hen when it appeared with 13 baby chicks.

As a joint project of the Alaska Native Brotherhood and the Alaska State Museum, Roberta designed and taught a cultural education program for children in Juneau, Alaska. There, she learned traditional skills from the elders and taught them to the young.

Roberta loves to folk dance, contra dance, and sing. She has sung with the San Francisco Symphony Chorus, the Oakland Symphony Chorus, and her family. She has taught rounds to elementary school students and has shared rounds with her friends and acquaintances all over the world. Recently, she performed in her twelfth opera with the Berkeley Opera Chorus, including singing from the top of a ladder!

AROUND THE WORLD WE GO!

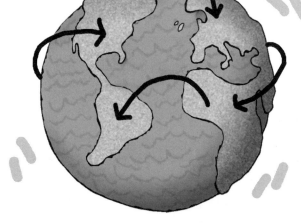

Ready to join me on an amazing adventure? You'll be traveling around the world (and even take a quick trip back in time!) to discover many of the diverse and fascinating cultures found all over the globe. Along the way, you'll see the creative ways different people live in their unique environments, and you'll celebrate the amazing art and crafts of many places as you re-create the toys, celebrations, music, art, furniture, and clothes of the people you meet.

Get ready to use your hands *and* your ideas! In many places the world over, and during much of history, people have made what they needed, using the materials they had at hand. We'll learn from their ingenuity as we find out how fun and rewarding it is to create things ourselves. I particularly love finding a way to make a traditional craft using something that our present-day culture throws away. Kids like you helped me come up with most of the ideas for re-creating the crafts in this book, so go ahead and figure out even better ways. I'd love to hear about your inventions and brilliant ideas!

I hope this book will convince you to have your own adventures both near and far. I have always loved to see new places and try new things. And the best part is not knowing what will happen next! When I traveled in Burma (in southeast Asia) in 1971, I met a group of beautiful young Burmese women — I was the first Westerner they had ever seen! Without any language in common, we had fun together. They took me to meet their friends and family, and played their traditional music for me. Then they asked me to teach them how to dance to rock and roll!

Here I am with the young women I met in Pagan, Burma. The two English phrases they knew were "rock and roll" and "I love you"!

After you've traveled around the world and arrived safely back home, close the book and look around at your family, friends, and neighbors. You might be surprised at how many countries and cultures are represented right in your own community! Maybe you are lucky enough to have parents and grandparents from several diverse parts of the world. And maybe someday you will travel and meet for yourself the friendly people of the world. I'm waiting to hear the stories of *your* multicultural adventures, near and far!

Start Saving Now!

No, not money for your trip — but things you might ordinarily throw away or toss into the recycling bin! These items will come in handy making crafts on your multicultural adventures!

- disposable aluminum pie pans and roasting pans
- plastic eggs
- old clothing: shoulder pads, long-sleeved shirts, worn-out sweatshirts or fleece jackets, jeans, clean white cotton T-shirts and handkerchiefs (great for dyeing), old pantyhose
- egg cartons
- small metal candy container or a lid from small metal container (such as a tea tin)
- wire spines from used-up spiral-bound notebooks
- black plastic-foam produce trays
- empty thread spools
- clothes hangers
- large plastic milk jugs
- string or yarn
- plastic coated wire (like old telephone wire)

MEXICO, THE WEST INDIES, & SOUTH AMERICA

We'll start our trip in sunny southern Mexico, make a swing through the Caribbean, and then head south! This region is a rich mix of native Indian (the Aztec, Maya, and Mixtec of Mexico and the Inca of Peru, among others), European (the Spanish explorers of the 1500s), and African cultures. The Spanish were able to conquer large areas because they had guns and horses for battle, and also because they unintentionally brought deadly diseases against which the local peoples had no defenses. Most of the Blacks were brought to this region as slaves. Today you'll find wonderful elements of all three cultures in the art, music, crafts, and traditions. Blacks are an especially important cultural influence in the Caribbean, where they have deeply influenced the music, language, and festivals.

Your first stop is in the state of Oaxaca, Mexico (1), to learn a traditional style of metalworking, a heritage of the Mixtec Indians. From there, you'll island-hop through the Caribbean to Barbados (2), where you'll make a sailor's valentine. In Venezuela (3), at the top of South America, you'll see the Spanish cultural influence directly when you decorate a traditional three-stick stool. Then, it's into the heart of the Amazon jungle (4) to make a gourd rattle. From there, hike over the Andes Mountains to Peru (5), where you'll weave a woolen pouch in an age-old Peruvian Indian style.

✹ Mexican Tin-Art Mirror

The Mixtec of Oaxaca, Mexico, made amazing metal jewelry and masks from the year 1200 until they were taken over by the Aztecs in the mid-1400s. They mined their own ore and made copper needles, rings, and bells. They then learned to melt together tin and copper to make bronze. By using extra tin, they created a metal that was golden in color, which they used to make images of the sun god. The Mixtec also melted together copper and arsenic, which looked silver and represented the moon god!

Metalwork is still popular in Mexico, and if you travel there now, you'll find mirrors decorated with tin flowers, animals, suns, moons, stars, and geometric designs. You will find beautiful tin angels, Aztec sun gods, birds, butterflies, cows, churches, crabs, crocodiles, donkeys, giraffes, lions, mermaids, parrots, people, roosters, stars, and swordfish, to name just a few! What design will you choose for *your* Mexican-style mirror?

WHAT YOU NEED

✳ Glue gun

✳ Small mirror

✳ Piece of wood or stiff cardboard 3" to 4" (7.5 to 10 cm) larger than the mirror on all sides

✳ Scissors

✳ Disposable aluminum pie pans or roasting pans

✳ Pencil

✳ Permanent markers (optional)

WHAT YOU DO

•**1**• Glue the mirror in the center of the wood or cardboard.

•**2**• Cut off the crimped edges of the aluminum pans so you have flat pieces. (Have an adult help you cut through the thick edges, if necessary.) With a pencil, draw whatever shapes you want onto the aluminum; cut them out. Be careful, because the edges may be sharp. Also, the little pieces that you snip off will be especially sharp, so be sure to throw them away carefully!)

•**3**• You can decorate the shapes with colorful permanent markers if you like. Use the markers in a well-ventilated place and don't rub the colors while they are wet. Once they are dry, the designs will be permanent.

•**4**• Glue the shapes onto the frame around the mirror.

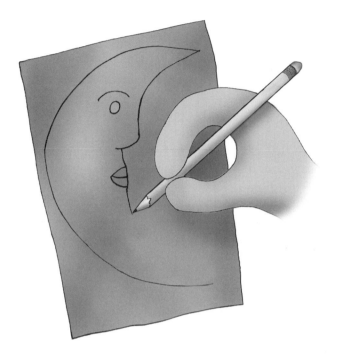

Aluminum is somewhat flexible, which makes it easy to create three-dimensional designs. I was taught how by a Mexican American child whose family was from Pueblo Tarimoro in the state of Guanajuato (gwa-na-HWA-to) in central Mexico. You need a soft cloth (such as a small towel) and a chopstick or Popsicle stick. Put your cutout metal shape upside down on the cloth. Push down and back and forth to indent the places that you want to have sticking up (eyes or the insides of ears, for example) when you turn the shape over.

✴ Sailor's Valentine from Barbados

In the 1800s, it was common for American sailors to bring presents home to their loved ones after being at sea for months — or sometimes even years! — at a time. They often bought the gifts on Barbados, one of a chain of tiny islands in the Caribbean Sea. The sailors were still a long way from their homes in New England, but the currents and winds made getting home from the West Indies, as these islands are called, relatively easy, so Barbados was their final stop.

The West Indian people used shells to create beautiful *mosaics* (raised patterns) of hearts and geometric shapes and phrases such as "With love," "Remember me when far away," and "Home again" to sell to the sailors. Traditionally these shell mosaics were made in hinged *octagonal* (eight-sided) wooden boxes and were about 3' (1 m) across! In the 1930s, the mosaics became known as "sailors' valentines."

Use shells, beads, and seeds to create a smaller version as a gift for a special friend!

WHAT YOU NEED

✴ Small metal candy or cough drop container, a lid from a small metal container (such as a tin for fancy tea), or a metal sardine can with the pull top cleanly removed

✴ Modeling clay

✴ Tiny shells; beads; sequins; small shell-shaped pasta; heart-shaped buttons; dried seeds of corn, sesame, red lentils; or beans

✴ Adhesive-backed paper (like Con-Tac paper)

✴ Stickers

WHAT YOU DO

•**1**• Cover the bottom of the metal container or lid with a layer of modeling clay.

•**2**• Press tiny shells, seeds, beads and other decorations into the wax. You can make abstract patterns or pictures or write a message to the recipient, or both!

•**3**• Cover the outside of the box with the adhesive paper and decorate it with stickers.

Crop Over!

At the end of July each year the people of Barbados celebrate Crop Over. Originally a one-day event from the 1800s to celebrate the end of the sugarcane harvest, it has grown into a month-long festival. From 1627 to 1966, the British controlled the country of Barbados and its sugarcane fields. Harvesting the cane was hard work, and the workers, who had been brought from Africa as slaves, celebrated when the last cart of canes was delivered to the mill. A worker would beat a gong to announce "Crop Over," which was followed by a donkey-cart parade and a day of dancing, music, wild costumes, and fun. One kind of music, called *tuk*, is a unique combination of African rhythms and British military music! You've probably heard of calypso, another Bajan musical style. Bajan (BAY-jun), meaning "of or from Barbados," is an example of the local dialect you would hear spoken in Barbados. It's a colorful mixture of island slang with British and African influences.

·YOU ARE HERE·

✴ Three-Stick Stool from Venezuela

When the Spanish explorers came to South America in the 1500s, they set up tents and furnished their temporary homes with simple furniture made of leather and wood. It was designed to be easily packed up and carried with them. When they settled permanently, they kept this simple style of furniture, but decorated the leather seats with beautiful carved designs, similar to the ornate leatherwork found on their horses' saddles.

You can make a comfy chair that folds up and is easy to take with you! Try this simplified technique to decorate it in the traditional style.

WHAT YOU NEED

✴ 3 strong sticks about 3' (1 m) long (old baseball bats are perfect!)

✴ Rope, about 3' (1 m)

✴ Denim from an old pair of jeans, 18" x 20" (45 x 50 cm)

✴ Chalk

✴ Yardstick (meter stick) or tape measure

✴ Scissors

✴ Fine-tip markers or fabric paint in tubes with applicator tips (dark colors look most authentic)

✴ Straight pins

✴ Sewing machine

WHAT YOU DO

•**1**• To tie the three sticks together, lay them next to each other and wind the rope loosely around a couple of times. Tie a double knot (page 116).

•**2**• Now spread out the three sticks evenly and try sitting on them! Even without the cloth seat, you can sit in the middle of the three sticks — the chair may settle a little, but if you tied the knot securely, it will hold you up.

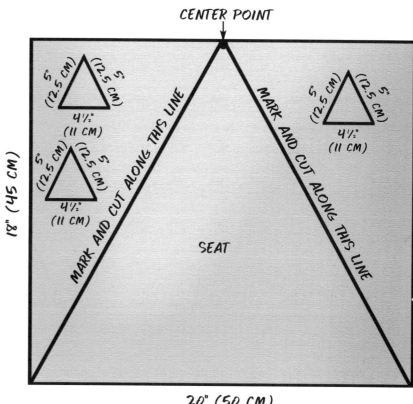

•**3**• To cut the cloth for the seat, fold the 18" (45 cm) sides of the denim together and mark the center point. Unfold and use the chalk and the yardstick to draw the two sides of the triangle as shown. Cut along the lines to form the seat. From the remaining material, cut three pockets for the three corners to hold the ends of the sticks.

CENTER POINT

5" (12.5 CM) 5" (12.5 CM)
4½" (11 CM)

5" (12.5 CM) 5" (12.5 CM)
4½" (11 CM)

5" (12.5 CM) 5" (12.5 CM)
4½" (11 CM)

18" (45 CM)

MARK AND CUT ALONG THIS LINE

MARK AND CUT ALONG THIS LINE

SEAT

20" (50 CM)

Around the World with Roberta

My first three-legged stool was a crazy design — a board with one wooden leg in the middle. My own legs were supposed to be the other two legs of the stool, creating a ... three-legged stool! I thought it was a wonderful idea and carried it out to the barn on Arminda's farm in Kentucky (page 112). I sat on it to milk the cow and immediately fell back into the muck-filled barnyard. I was a mess — but I didn't spill the milk!

Try Leather Stamping!

Leather carving or tooling is an ancient art — the Moors brought it from the Middle East to Spain and the Spanish brought it to Latin America. It requires much practice to learn the technique of carving three-dimensional designs into leather. An easier way to decorate leather is called stamping. The artist places a metal shape on the leather and hammers an impression of it into the leather. Ask a local leather goods or shoe repair store if you could have a scrap of leather. Dampen it slightly. Use a small hammer and whatever metal shapes you can think of (nail, Phillips-head screwdriver, bolt, or metal bottle cap) to make your own designs.

•4• Decorate the seat with fine-tip markers or fabric paint. The fabric paint will give you a raised texture that looks a little like real tooling. The real designs are very intricate!

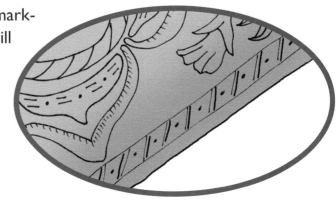

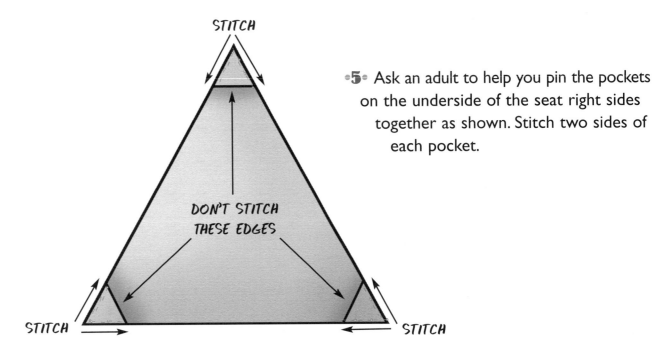

STITCH

DON'T STITCH THESE EDGES

STITCH

STITCH

•5• Ask an adult to help you pin the pockets on the underside of the seat right sides together as shown. Stitch two sides of each pocket.

•6• Reverse the pockets and slip the ends of the sticks into them. Now, have a seat! Isn't it surprisingly comfortable? If the chair is too low and the legs are splaying out too far, remove the seat and retie the knot so it's farther down the legs. Fold up your stool, take it outside, and sit and watch the world go by!

Amazon Basin Gourd Rattle

The second longest river in the world, the Amazon flows from the Andes Mountains in Peru across Brazil to the Atlantic Ocean. The Amazon basin (the area drained by the river and its tributaries) is home to many native peoples who have lived deep within this huge tropical rain forest for thousands of years.

One of the cultural traditions these diverse peoples share is the crafting of beautifully decorated rattles made from dried gourds (the seeds rattle in the hollow interior). The Wai Wai and the Piaroa, for example, etch the hard outer surface of the gourd with intricate designs. Some rattles are used in music and dance celebrations; others are important in sacred ceremonies and in the rituals of a *shaman* (tribal healer).

You can decorate your rattles with some of the amazing animals of the Amazon basin!

Amazing Amazonia!

Amazonia, as the Amazon basin is also called, is home to more than 2,000 species of fish, 600 mammals, and *two million* different types of insects, many of which aren't found anywhere else in the world! Some of the many amazing animals you'll find in this region are anacondas and boas (two types of snakes), jaguars and three-toed sloths, tapirs and peccaries (they look something like a wild pig), toucans and parrots, spider monkeys and tree frogs.

WHAT YOU NEED

* *Papier-mâché supplies:* large bowl; 3 cups (750 ml) water; 1½ cups (375 ml) flour; wire whisk; old newspaper, torn into small pieces; newspaper sheets (to protect your work surface)

* Blown (no longer working) incandescent lightbulb

* Masking tape

* Acrylic paint (raw sienna color, available at an art supply store, dries to the perfect golden gourd color)

* Paintbrush

* Fine-point roller-ball pens such as Uniball (black will look the most authentic)

* Reference book with drawings or photos of animals from the Amazon basin

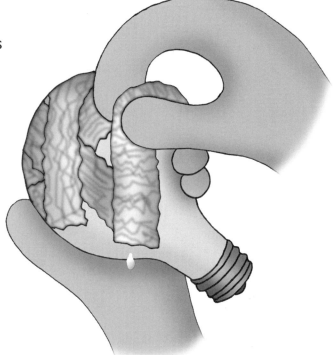

WHAT YOU DO

To make the papier-mâché paste
Pour the water into the bowl. Gradually add the flour to the water, ½ cup (125 ml) at a time and whisk it until it's smooth.

To make the rattle

•**1**• Remove any jewelry you're wearing and roll up your sleeves. Cover your work surface with newspaper.

•**2**• Dip a strip of newspaper into the paste. Wrap it around the lightbulb. Continue dipping and wrapping strips until you have covered the bulb completely with at least five layers of papier-mâché. Try to make it smooth. Let it dry completely.

•**3**• Throw the dry rattle onto the floor once or twice to crack the glass inside, but try not to dent or break the papier-mâché covering. If you get a small hole or crack, cover it carefully with several pieces of masking tape. Shake your rattle to see how good it sounds!

•**4**• Paint the entire rattle and let it dry. Use the permanent markers to decorate with animal designs.

My nephew brought this gourd rattle back from Peru. Covered with intricate designs, it is dated and signed by the artist, Sonia Seguil Garcia.

A "Rattler" for Your Rattle!

Draw the head and forked tongue of a rattlesnake on the narrow end of the rattle, then draw the coiled diamond-backed snake body around and around on the bulb. End with the rattles around the bottom. The older a rattlesnake gets, the more rattles at the tail, so exaggerate if you want!

The People of the Amazon

Many Amazon natives are increasingly coming into contact with the outside world. The Yagua people, for example, live in the western Amazon, near the border of Colombia and Peru. The Yagua use dried calabash fruits (similar to a dried gourd) to make beautifully decorated dolls, bowls, and masks. When a group of tourists is scheduled to come to the village to trade for handcrafted items, the Yagua wear their traditional skirts made of palm fibers. When the tourists aren't around, they wear jeans, shorts, and other modern-day clothing!

Wonder what it would be like to grow up in the Amazon rainforest? Check out this web-site <**www.junglephotos.com/people/ children/children.html**> to see photos of kids from some of the less remote villages. You'll see them playing soccer (make that "futbol"!), swimming, sitting in a classroom, climbing trees, playing with their pets, and helping with household chores. Sound familiar?

✺ Peruvian Woven Pouch

The native Peruvians (the people who were living in what is now Peru when the Spanish arrived) have been weaving for thousands of years. The Paracas people on the southern coast of Peru, for example, were weaving intricate and colorful items more than 2,500 years ago. Peruvians are still known for their beautiful weaving. Their looms are made of wood, but you'll use cardboard and wind the string on in a special way that allows you to weave around and around to create a traditional men's pouch with no seams! Called a *ch'uspa* (CHUS-pa) in the Quechuan language, these pouches are traditionally made in bright colors and decorated with pom-poms.

WHAT YOU NEED

✳ Scissors

✳ Cardboard piece, about 5" x 6" (12.5 x 15 cm)

✳ Strong thin yarn or string for the lengthwise strings (the warp)

✳ Thick yarn* for the "around and around" strings (the weft)

✳ 3 pieces of colorful yarn about 12' (3.5 m)

✳ Needle and yarn or thick thread

✳ Thin yarn for pom-poms (optional)

*It's important to use *thick* yarn for the weft. Otherwise, the project will take too long and you might get discouraged!

The Kids' Multicultural Craft Book

WHAT YOU DO

To make the loom

Cut the cardboard on the top and bottom as shown to the right to make 10 slits on the 5" (12.5 cm) side.

To string the warp

This process only sounds complicated! Ask an adult to help you get started.

•**1**• Cut 10' (3 m) of string or strong thin yarn. Tie the end of the string to the top notch on the left side of the piece of cardboard.

•**2**• Here is the stringing sequence:

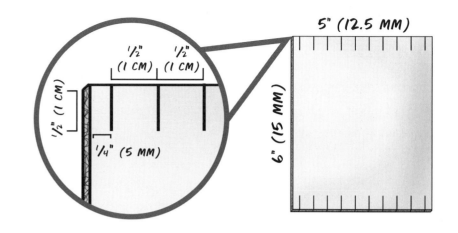

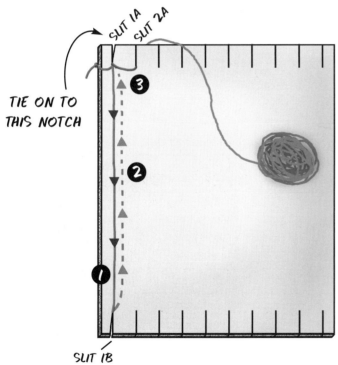

Bring the string down the front from slit 1A on top through slit 1B at the bottom. Go up on the back side and through slit 1A again. Bring the string across from 1A to slit 2A in front as shown.

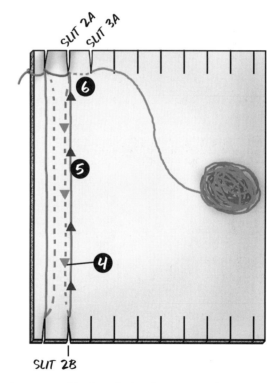

Bring the string down in back of the loom and through slit 2B on the bottom. Take the string up the front through slit 2A again. Bring the string across from slit 2A to slit 3A in back.

•**3**• Repeat the stringing sequence, using slits 3A, 3B, and 4A. Continue repeating until you have worked your way across the top and bottom.

•**4**• After you go up and through 10A to complete the last sequence, bring the string down on the back and tie a knot in the end next to 10B. This creates an *uneven* number of warp threads so that the in and out weaving of the weft thread will alternate on each row.

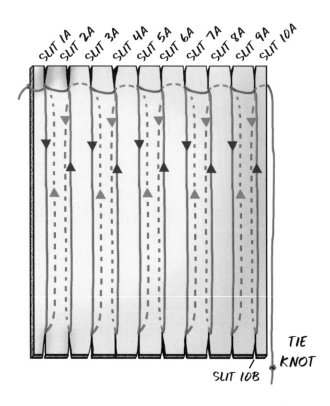

SLIT 1A SLIT 2A SLIT 3A SLIT 4A SLIT 5A SLIT 6A SLIT 7A SLIT 8A SLIT 9A SLIT 10A

TIE KNOT

SLIT 10B

To weave the weft
This is the easy part!
•**1**• Tie the thick yarn to the first warp string at the bottom. Weave it in and out of the warp strings, going under one, over one, under one, over one, and so on. Weave across the front of the cardboard, across the back, and then across the front again.

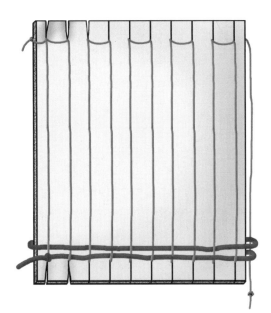

•**2**• Continue weaving around and around the cardboard loom. Every once in a while, push the weaving down tightly so your pouch will be thick. Weave all the way to the top.

•**3**• Remove the cardboard loom by bending the cardboard slits at the top and slipping off the string loops. Pull the cardboard loom out through the top and *ta-da!* — a pouch with no seams!

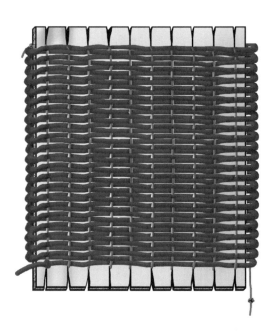

To make the handle

•**1**• Tie the three pieces of yarn to the back of a chair or to a doorknob. Hold the loose ends and twist the yarn over and over until it is tight.

•**2**• Have a friend grab the middle of the twisted yarn and hold it straight while you bring the loose ends back to the tied ends.

•**3**• Hold all the ends together while your friend lets go. Suddenly the yarn will twist together, forming a strong rope about 5' (1.5 m) long. Cut the three tied ends. Use a double knot (page 116) to tie them to the loose ends you were holding.

•**4**• Whipstitch (page 118) your handle onto the sides of the bag.

•**5**• Add pom-poms!

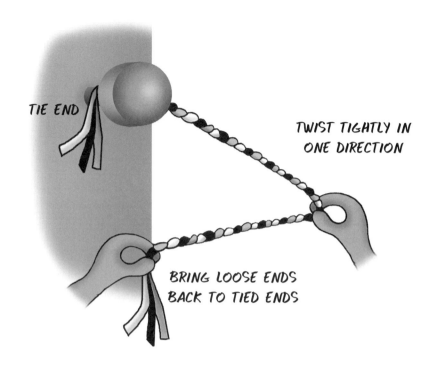

TIE END

TWIST TIGHTLY IN ONE DIRECTION

BRING LOOSE ENDS BACK TO TIED ENDS

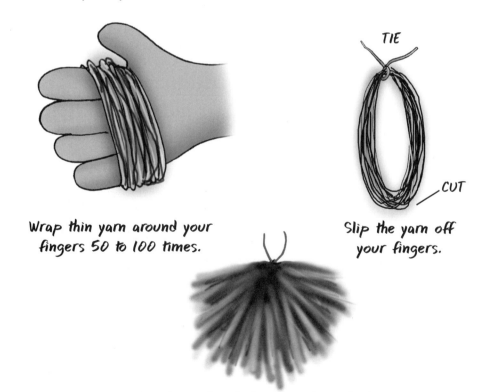

Wrap thin yarn around your fingers 50 to 100 times.

TIE

CUT

Slip the yarn off your fingers.

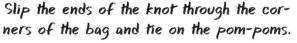

Slip the ends of the knot through the corners of the bag and tie on the pom-poms.

•SINCE LONG AGO•

Quechua (qhesh-wa), the language of the ancient Incas, is still spoken in many parts of South America! In fact, about a quarter of the population of Peru speaks it, although the majority of those people also speak Spanish. If you listen to Andean music, you will hear some songs sung in Quechua!

AFRICA

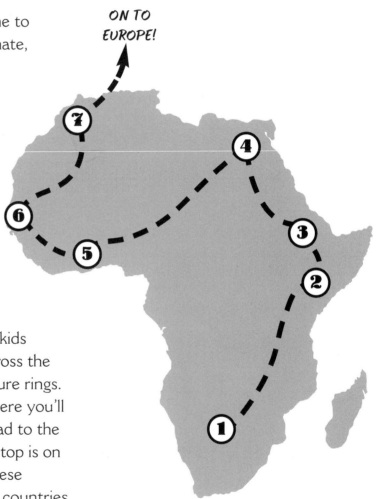

ON TO EUROPE!

This huge continent, with both modern cities and traditional villages, is home to hundreds of distinct ethnic groups. Isolated in many cases by geography, climate, and sheer distance, many of these native peoples still live very traditional lifestyles, reflected in their crafts and cultural traditions.

Even though Africa straddles the equator, much of it is not as terribly hot as you might expect, thanks to western coastal breezes as well as the higher elevations in the east. All across northern Africa, however, is the huge Sahara Desert, where it can reach 130°F (54°C) during the day. The Kalahari is a smaller, less inhospitable desert in the south. The ancestors of the San, who inhabit the Kalahari, are probably the ancestors of us all!

The Kalahari is where you will start your African adventures, in the country of Botswana (1), where in the tradition of the San people you'll make (and decorate) an ostrich egg! When you arrive in Kenya (2), I hope you are ready to race your *garimoto*, a handmade toy car popular with kids here. In Ethiopia (3), you'll need a pair of Shangalla sand shoes so you can cross the desert into Egypt (4), where you'll travel back in time to make scarab signature rings. Put those sand shoes back on and cross the Sahara Desert to Ghana (5), where you'll make a talking drum, used to communicate between villages. Next you'll head to the tiny West African nation of Gambia (6) to make a traditional doll. Your last stop is on the northern coast. Isolated from the rest of the continent by the Sahara, these countries reflect the cultural influence of the southern European and Arabic countries just across the Mediterranean Sea, as shown by the Moroccan (7) hand pendant you'll make here — a good luck charm for the rest of your trip!

Ostrich-Egg Water Holder from the Kalahari Desert

The San people who live in the Kalahari Desert in southern Africa use large, strong ostrich eggshells for water storage. They make a small hole in the shell (so they can eat the egg). Then they draw personal symbols on the eggs to show ownership. During the rainy season, they fill the eggs with water and store them near their homes. They also carry them on food-foraging journeys, often burying eggshells full of water on the way out so they have water for the trip back.

Each shell is decorated with different patterns scratched into the surface and colored with red and black paint. The designs are similar to the ancient rock art found in many places in southern Africa. Geometric patterns include dots, zigzags, spirals, hatching and crosshatching, and images are typically humans, birds, snakes, and antelope.

You can decorate your papier-mâché ostrich egg any way you like!

The Awesome Ostrich!

Native to central and southern Africa, ostriches are the largest living birds. They can be 8' (2.5 m) tall! Ostrich eggs have to be strong because the mom weighs over 300 pounds (150 kg) and she has to sit on them! Ostrichs can't fly but they can run up to 40 mph (64 kph) when a predator is chasing them.

You may have heard the term *African bushmen.* This is what the Europeans called the native people they found living in the "bush," the sparsely settled desert. Properly called the San, this ethnic group has lived in the Kalahari region for thousands of years. Many still follow the traditional hunting and gathering culture of their ancestors. Rock paintings show early San people hunting ostriches by disguising themselves as ostriches so they could get close enough to shoot with their small bows and arrows. The ostrich-shell water holder is just one example of the many ingenious ways the San have adapted to life in the desert!

You can see some of the ancient rock paintings of the San at <**www.rhino.org.za/kamberg_rockart.htm**>. Anthropologists and historians are only just beginning to understand the deeper spiritual meaning this rock art had for the San people.

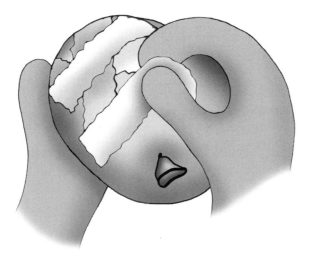

WHAT YOU NEED

* *Papier-mâché supplies:* large bowl; 3 cups (750 ml) water; 1¹/₂ cups (375 ml) flour; wire whisk; tan or white construction paper, torn into small pieces; newspaper sheets (to protect your work surface)
* Balloon
* Pens and colored pencils, black and red

WHAT YOU DO

To make the papier-mâché paste
Pour the water into the bowl. Gradually add the flour to the water, ¹/₂ cup (125 ml) at a time and whisk it until it's smooth.

To make the egg
•**1**• Blow up the balloon. (An ostrich egg is typically about 6"/15 cm long and 5"/12.5 cm wide.) Remove any jewelry you're wearing and roll up your sleeves. Cover your work surface with newspaper.

•**2**• Dip a piece of paper into the paste and press it on the balloon. Continue dipping and placing pieces until you have covered the balloon with several layers, leaving a small hole at the knotted end. Let it dry thoroughly in the sun or in a warm room for a day. When dry, pop the balloon. You'll have a small hole like the opening in the traditional water shell.

•**3**• Decorate with pens and pencils.

Kenyan Garimoto, or "Hot Car"

Kids living in the countryside and small towns in Kenya, in eastern Africa, make these toy cars out of scrap wire and metal. In Swahili, these cars are called *garimoto* — *gari* is "car" and *moto* is "hot" or "fiery." (By "hot," they mean "cool!") The kids each try to get their little car to run as smoothly and evenly as possible. Then they all get together to have races. These homemade toy cars are very popular in many parts of Africa — maybe you'll start a new trend where you live!

WHAT YOU NEED

* Needle-nose pliers
* Yardstick (meter stick) or measuring tape
* Wire that is flexible but strong enough to hold its shape: 26" (65 cm) of 16- or 18-gauge wire for the back wheels and axle; 18" (45 cm) of thinner wire for the frame
* Can that is about 2³/₄" (7 cm) high, with circumference of about 9" (22.5 cm)
* Empty thread spool
* Plastic-coated wire (from a craft store) or old telephone wire in many colors for decoration (optional)
* Wire clothes hanger
* Wire cutters
* Small box or plastic container for the compartment of the car

The unraveled wire spine of a used-up spiral-bound notebook works great for the front axle and car frame. Telephone wire is great for decorating your car but can be a little tricky to find. If you live near a recycle or reuse depot (often located near a recycling center), you can probably find some colorful wire there. Or you can use plastic-coated or colored craft wire from a craft or hobby shop.

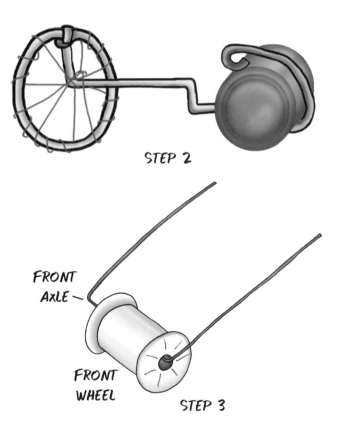

STEP 2

FRONT AXLE

FRONT WHEEL

STEP 3

WHAT YOU DO

•**1**• Use the pliers to bend each end of the 26" (65 cm) piece of flexible wire over ¼" (5 mm). Measure 9" (22.5 cm) from each end and mark it by bending the wire in those two places. Measure another 1¼" (3 cm) in from there and bend again.

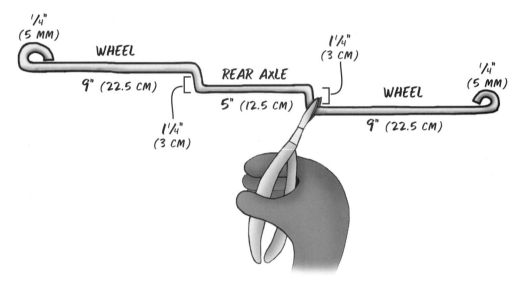

¼" (5 MM)

WHEEL

9" (22.5 CM)

1¼" (3 CM)

REAR AXLE

5" (12.5 CM)

1¼" (3 CM)

WHEEL

9" (22.5 CM)

¼" (5 MM)

•**2**• Form one 9" (22.5 cm) section into a circle by wrapping it around the can.

Slip it off and loop the end of the wire over the bend to secure the circle. Use the pliers to press the loop closed. Repeat with the other 9" (22.5 cm) section.

Try rolling your wheels — you may need to adjust the shape so they roll smoothly.

Use the colorful wire to add spokes to the wheels or to decorate them, if you want. But don't wrap anything around the axle or it won't roll.

•**3**• Slip the spool onto the thinner plastic-coated wire, and bend the wire to form an axle for the front wheel.

•4• Loop the ends of the wires around the back axle, tight enough to stay in place but loose enough for the axle to turn.

•5• To make the hanger into a pushing stick, cut off a section that includes the hook at the top. Hook the other end around the rear axle, and press it closed with the pliers. Use the hook as a handle as shown on the finished car.

•6• Make a seat in your car with a small box, piece of fabric, or whatever you have around.

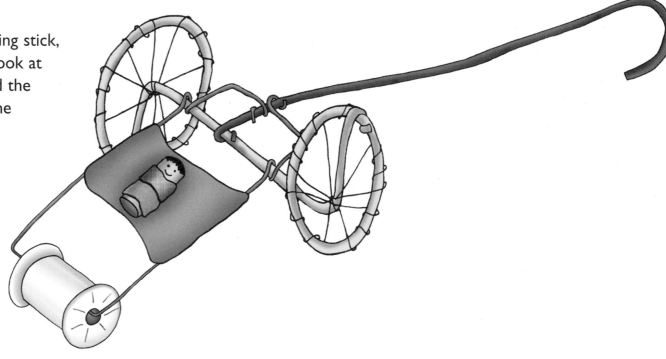

Around the World with Roberta

The African friend who taught me how to make the garimoto is from a village in Kenya, where the Rare (RAH-ray) River drains into the Indian Ocean. He loved growing up next to the river and swimming there. Once a year the river would overflow its banks, but that made everyone happy because the water brought the fish up into the fields where they could be easily gathered in the shallow water! After the water lowered again, it left behind rich silt (fine particles from the river bottom) that improved the soil so the next crops grew abundantly. Unfortunately in 1982, a European company dammed the river and built a factory that has polluted the water. In 1997, very heavy rains in that area washed away the dam, but the company is rebuilding it.

✳ Shangalla Sand Shoes from Ethiopia

African people who lived near or traveled through the huge Sahara Desert in northern Africa devised different styles of special shoes for walking in the sand. They typically made their sandals wider and longer than their feet, a cool idea that works very much like snowshoes. The shoes keep you from sinking into the sand and having to work extra hard to walk.

The Shangalla of Ethiopia make sandals of leather stitched with interesting patterns. To make it easy to walk quickly through loose sand, the heel is wide and has a tail, and the toe is upturned!

Make a pair of Shangalla sandals so you can stride across the top of the sand.

WHAT YOU NEED

✳ *Pattern-making supplies:* pencil, tracing paper, craft scissors, manila folder or heavy paper

✳ Piece of rug pad from a carpet/rug store (the strong quilted type is perfect), at least 16" x 20" (40 x 50 cm)

✳ Fabric scissors

✳ Four 10" (27.5 cm) pieces of wire (each about the thickness of a bicycle spoke)

✳ Packing tape or masking tape

✳ Permanent markers

✳ 2 shoelaces or 12" (30 cm) pieces of ribbon or leather

WHAT YOU DO

•**1**• Trace the SAND SHOE pattern (pages 123 to 124) onto tracing paper. Cut out the two pieces and tape them together to make a full-size pattern. Now trace the tracing-paper pattern onto the manila folder or heavy paper and cut it out. Label the pattern.

•**2**• Place the paper pattern on the rug pad and trace around it two times. Cut both shoes out carefully.

•**3**• Tape the wires onto the soles as shown.

•**4**• Step on the soles and starting just beyond your toes, bend the wires up almost 90° so that the toes of the shoes point up. (Ask for adult help if you need it.)

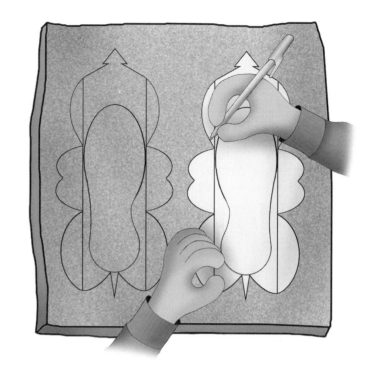

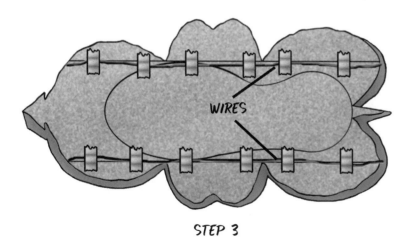

WIRES

STEP 3

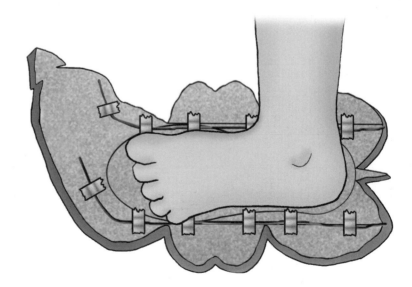

STEP 4

•**5**• With the permanent markers, decorate your shoes in interesting patterns.

•**6**• Use the shoelaces to tie each shoe on your foot by going under the sandal, across your foot and back under, then across higher up (toward your ankle). Try out your sandals on a giant sand dune or in the nearest sandbox!

Turned-Up Toes!

There are lots of kinds of shoes with turned-up toes! The ancient Egyptians wore a similar style of sandals woven from *rushes* (riverside grasses). *Opanki,* leather dancing shoes of Serbia and Bulgaria, and traditional Turkish embroidered and beaded slippers both have turned-up toes. Kids in Tuva (in Siberia) wear shoes with turned-up toes so they don't disturb the earth, which they believe is sacred. Even modern snowshoes are made that way so it's easier to trudge through deep snow. If you've never walked in shoes with turned-up toes, you'll finally get to see what it feels like!

Egyptian Scarab Ring

The ancient Egyptians were fascinated by the scarab beetle and made many carvings of this insect. Scarab beetles are also called *dung beetles* because they live in manure. The Egyptians considered them a symbol of life and rebirth.

Many scarab carvings were less than 1" (2.5 cm) long and were worn on rings. Some carved scarabs were mounted on a swivel ring with special carvings on the back that were used as a signature seal. The seal would be pressed into warm wax, soft leather or clay, creating an impression of the engraving. The engraving was usually a personal symbol, or the person's name. Sometimes the bottom side of the scarab was engraved with words (in Egyptian hieroglyphics, of course) or decorative animal shapes. If you visit a museum with a collection of Egyptian artifacts, see if it has any scarab rings.

Design your own personal signature symbol for your scarab ring!

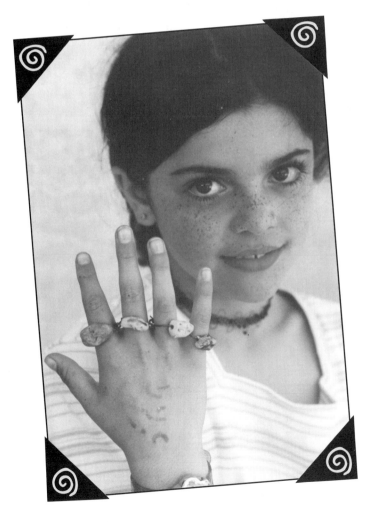

WHAT YOU NEED

* Air-drying or polymer clay in several colors (CHOOSING A CLAY, page 114)
* Knitting needle or kitchen skewer
* Nail or round toothpick
* Paper and pencil
* Colorful wire, 4" (10 cm): use colored craft wire, or recycled wire (page 26)
* Candle and matches (use with adult help)

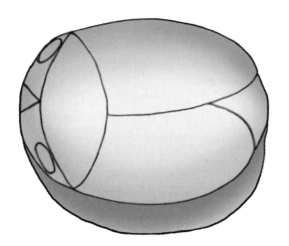

SCARAB BEETLE

WHAT YOU DO

To make the scarab

•1• Shape a small amount of the clay into a scarab beetle. Make it less than 1" (2.5 cm) long. Be sure to make the top rounded and the bottom totally flat.

•2• Use the knitting needle or skewer to make a hole through the clay beetle as shown.

•3• Use the nail or toothpick to make your own personal symbol on the flat bottom of the beetle. Simple patterns work the best. The marks should be about the depth and width of a raw spaghetti noodle. Important! Remember to make letters and words *backwards*, because when you press the ring into warm wax, everything will come out the opposite of what you have formed! Practice by writing it on a piece of paper; then check it in a mirror.

•4• If using polymer clay, ask an adult to bake the beetles for you according to the package directions. They can be baked on the skewer like shish kebabs or just put in a pan. Otherwise, let them air-dry.

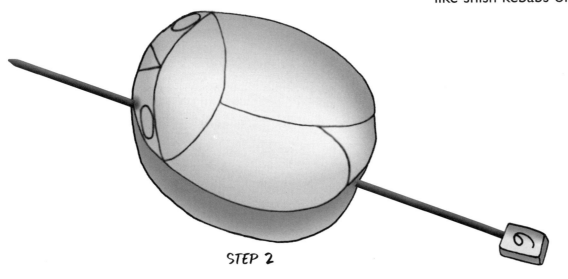

STEP 2

STEP 3

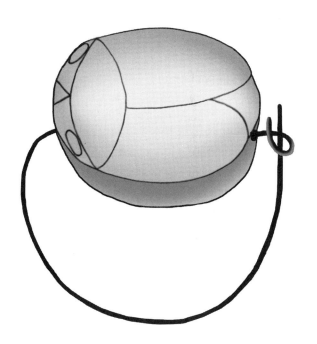

To make the ring

•1• Shape the ring by making a small loop in one end of the wire. Feed the other end through the scarab. Bend it into a ring and slip the end through the loop.

•2• Try the ring on and pull the wire until the ring fits. If you make it loose-fitting, you can turn it while it's on your finger; otherwise, you'll have to slip the ring off to reposition the scarab. When you have whichever fit you want, slip off the ring, cut off all but ½" (1 cm) of the extra wire and twist it securely around the ring.

•3• Put the ring on and turn it so that the signature side shows. Light the candle and drip some wax on the paper. Let the wax cool a bit, then push the flat side of the ring into the wax. Isn't that cool?

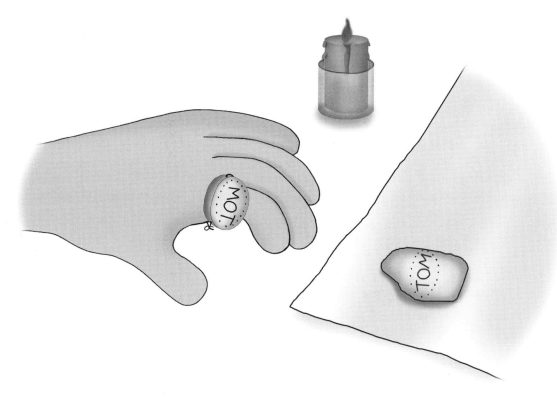

Scarab Colors

Scarab rings were made of clay, pure gold, or colorful gemstones such as greenstone, turquoise, lapis lazuli (bluish violet), amethyst (purplish violet), obsidian (black), or soapstone (whitish). So use your most colorful clays!

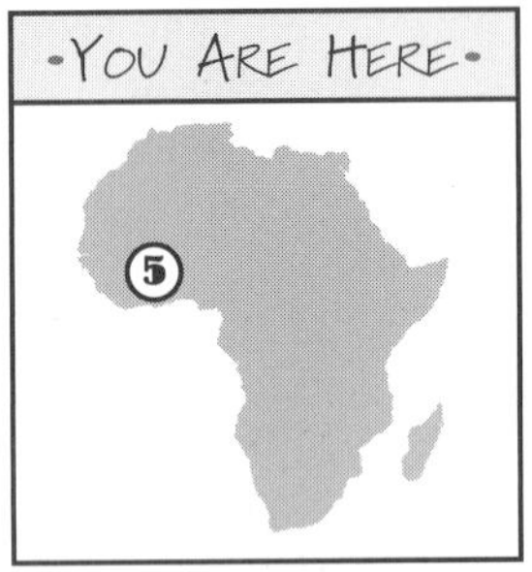

Talking Drum from Ghana

Drums have been used all over Africa for thousands of years to communicate across distances. They can be very useful to warn of danger, for example. As telephones are becoming more commonplace in rural Africa, the knowledge of the special drum languages is, sadly, being lost.

This kind of drum can be made to "talk" by squeezing the lengthwise strings. The tighter they are squeezed, the tighter the drumhead becomes and the higher the sound.

Here are two versions, one easy and one a little more challenging (but more authentic). You choose!

What You Need

* 2 disposable latex gloves (for the easy version) or rawhide (for the more challenging version), available at a leather or craft store
* 2 small clay flowerpots, about 11" (27.5 cm) in diameter (or larger)
* Pencil or pen
* Scissors
* 6' to 9' (1.5 to 2.5 m) of rawhide thong (most authentic-looking), thin string, or very thin rope
* Needle with a large eye (if you are using string)

WHAT YOU DO

Easy version

•1• Pull a glove over the top of each clay pot.

•2• Place the two pots on top of each other with the small ends together and tie the fingers and thumbs of one glove to those of the other glove around the outside of the pots. When you have tied it tightly enough, your drumheads will have an amazingly beautiful sound. Try holding the drum in different ways and experiment to see what different kinds of sounds you can make.

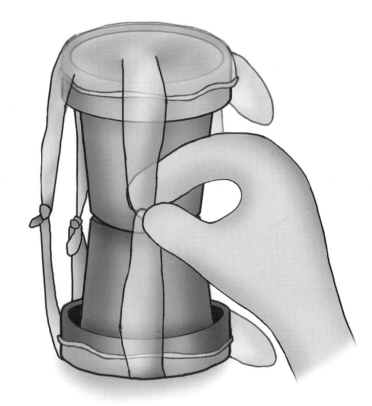

Crafty Idea! You can buy a rawhide thong — or you can make one from a piece of rawhide! It is so stretchy and strong, it can be pulled really tight without breaking.

Soak a round piece of rawhide in water overnight. Starting at the outside, cut a ¹/₂" (1 cm) spiral into the center of the piece. Pull on it and it will straighten into a long thong.

More challenging version

•**1**• Trace the tops of your clay pots onto the rawhide and draw another circle 1" (2.5 cm) larger around it. Cut the rawhide on the outer circles.

•**2**• Soak the rawhide in water overnight so it will be stretchy when you work with it.

•**3**• With the points of the scissors, snip small holes every 2" (5 cm) around the rawhide circles, ¹/₂" (1 cm) in from the edge. A grown-up helper is handy to make sure the holes go in just the right places!

•**4**• Lay one circle of rawhide on the table and place one clay pot upside down on top. Set the other clay pot and the other circle of rawhide on top as shown.

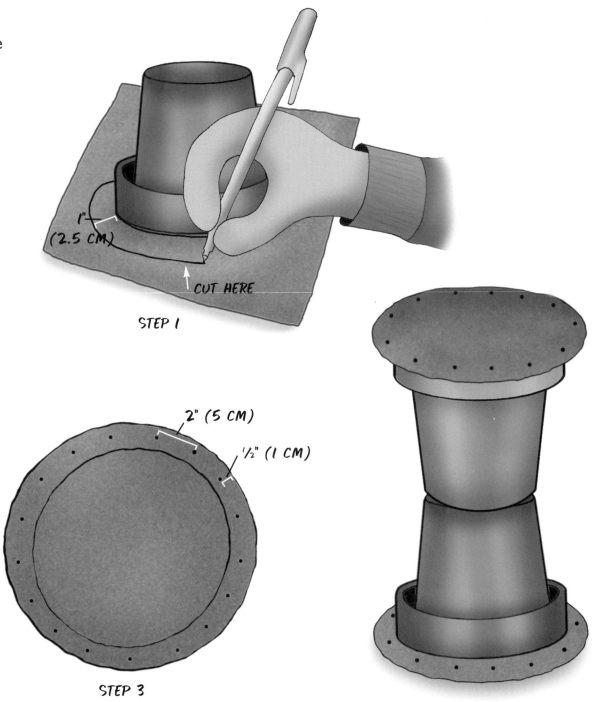

1"
(2.5 CM)

↑ CUT HERE

STEP 1

2" (5 CM)

¹/₂" (1 CM)

STEP 3

STEP 4

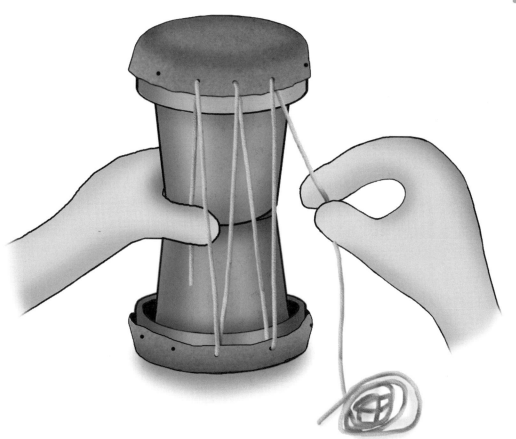

•5• It's handy to have a friend help you hold the pots and the end of the string in place during this step. If you are using string, it is much easier if you thread it on a needle first. Lace the rope through a hole in the top rawhide circle and then through a hole in the bottom circle. Continue in a zigzag pattern from the top pot to the bottom and back to the top all the way around the pots.

•6• Tighten the string by pulling up on one "zig" and down on the next "zag," working your way around the drum. The tighter the drumhead, the better the sound.

•7• When the rawhide is tight enough, tie the two ends together and cut off the excess.

When your drum is dry (the drumhead will tighten as it dries and make an even better sound!), it's ready to play!

The Language of Drums

Many African languages are tonal, which means the words are spoken in a song-like way, with individual words rising and falling in tone. It would be hard to drum these tonal sounds, so communities invented longer phrases to be drummed for each word. In the Lokele language of the upper Congo (the region surrounding the Congo River in central Africa), for example, *ngwa* (dog) is drummed out with the tones of "giant dog, little one that barks 'kpei kpci'."

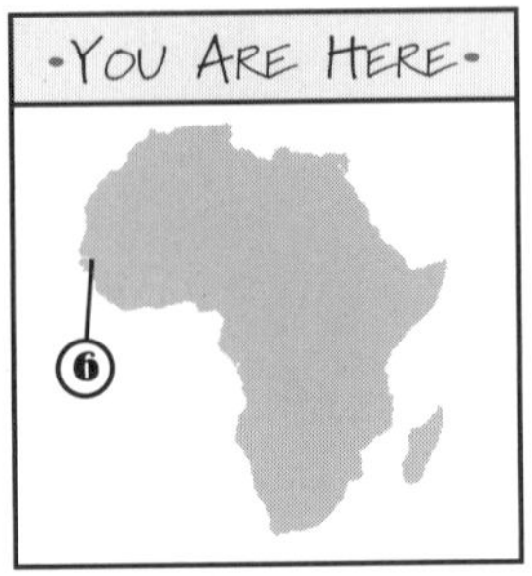

Gambian Doll in Traditional Attire

In the West Africa nation of Gambia, the markets are a colorful place to visit full of beautifully dressed people. The women wear head wraps and full-length loose-fitting clothing in wonderful patterns and colors. They often carry their young children on their backs, using a piece of colorful cloth. Men wear traditional shirts like a *dashiki* or a *kitenge* made of tie-dyed cloth or other fabric styles decorated in wonderful patterns and colors. Some Africans wear Western-style clothes for everyday wear and save their traditional clothing for celebrations and other special days.

You'll find dolls similar to this one for sale in the marketplaces of West Africa. You can even make your own tie-dyed cloth for her traditional outfit and head wrap. Or you can use a favorite piece of colorful cloth — to reflect the variety of fabrics used in Africa!

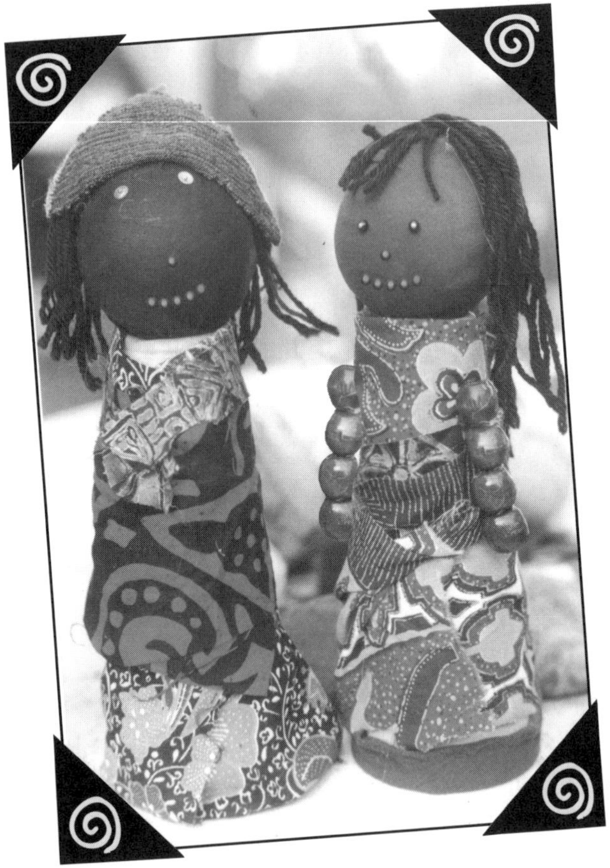

Greetings from Gambia!

Africa's smallest country, Gambia is a narrow strip of land on the western coast that is almost entirely surrounded by Senegal. It is downwind from the vast Sahara, so sometimes the sun is obscured for days on end from fine dust that is blown into the air when the winds blow fiercely in the desert thousands of miles (km) away!

WHAT YOU NEED

* Old tennis ball or plastic-foam ball
* Black or brown knee-high stocking or the knee and foot section from an old pair of pantyhose
* Rubber band
* Paper-towel tube, cardboard cone left over from yarn or string (ask at a weaving or knitting store), or very tall paper cup
* Scissors
* Glue gun
* Yarn (unraveled black sweaters or socks make curly hair)
* Permanent markers
* Tiny beads and short pins or ball-point pins (with a colorful ball on the end)
* 2 craft sticks or 2 short sections of wire and brown wooden beads
* Pieces of colorful cloth

Try a Wrap!

Many West African women wear head wraps as protection against the hot sun. Try it on your doll — or on yourself! Wrapping a cloth around your head to make a kind of hat is lots of fun, and at the website <**www.Africaimports.com**>, they show you how to do it. Click on "Free Articles" and then on "How to put on a headwrap."

WHAT YOU DO

To make the doll

•**1**• Cover the ball with the stocking to give the doll dark skin. Here's the easiest way to do this: Hold the ball in your hand. Pull the stocking onto your hand until the ball is in the toe, then pull your hand out.

Wind the rubber band around the stocking close to the ball. Pull the stocking back over the ball to make two layers so the ball doesn't show through.

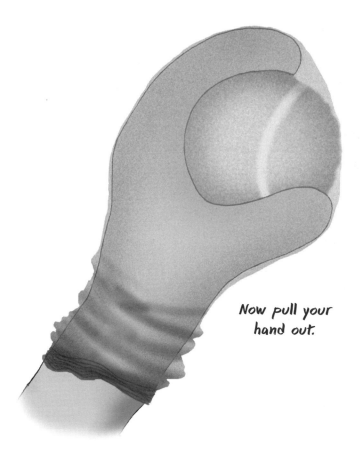

Now pull your hand out.

Africa 39

SNIP SMALL
SLIT HERE

STEP 2

•2• To hold the head onto the body, pull the end of the stocking down through the top of the tube or cone and back up over the outside. Or, if using a paper cup, make a small slit in the bottom of the cup and pull the end of the stocking through, then pull the stocking back up over the outside. (To form the body of the doll, the cup will be upside down.)

•3• Glue on yarn for hair and draw on a face. You can make eyes with small beads and pins as shown or just use the ball-point pins.

•4• Cut a small piece of cloth and use it for a traditional head wrap. Use the remainder to wrap your doll in a long, loose-fitting dress, tying the corners around the tube to hold the dress in place.

•5• For the arms, use craft sticks or string beads on wires, then glue them to the body. If they won't stay, try poking a small hole on each side of the body so you can push the arms through and then glue them in place.

Dye a Traditional Outfit!

All over Africa, the most common way to make patterns on cloth is to dye only certain parts of it. With tie-dye, for example, you fold or bunch small sections of the cloth and then tie up the bunched places to keep the dye from coloring those areas. With a package of fabric dye and a piece of cotton cloth, you can create a traditional outfit for your doll. Or try batik (page 81), which is also traditional in Africa. In fact, a commonly used dye is blue indigo, also used in Java!

Moroccan Hand Pendant

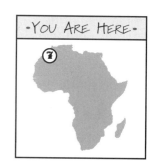
This hanging charm is called a *hamsa* (HAHM-sah, Arabic for the number 5) or *hamesh* (HA-mash, for the five books that comprise the Torah) to refer to the five fingers of the hand. The hand shape is typically a stylized version with the fingers and thumb all the same length or with a very curved thumb. Sometimes the hand even has two thumbs with only three fingers in between!

These *amulets* (protective charms) are traditionally made of silver or brass, elaborately etched with flowers, leaves, tendrils, and birds. They may be decorated with a Jewish six-sided star or a special protective eye. They are still used for good luck by Muslims, Christians, and Jews.

WHAT YOU NEED

* Old newspapers
* Scissors
* Disposable aluminum pie pan or roasting pan
* Scrap paper (optional)
* Pencil
* Small nail
* Hole punch (optional)
* Yarn or string

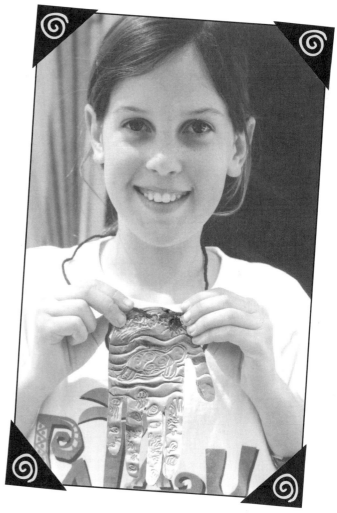

WHAT YOU DO

•**1**• Spread out the newspapers to protect your work surface. Cut off the crimped edges of the aluminum pan so you have a flat piece.

•**2**• Decide if you want to make a stylized hand shape (see the example on the right) or if you want to trace your own hand. You can practice your stylized design on a piece of scrap paper; then put the paper on the aluminum and trace over the lines with the pencil to indent the metal underneath. If using your own hand, trace it directly onto the aluminum.

•**3**• Cut out the hand shape carefully. The aluminum edges become sharp when cut, so be careful! (Ask for adult help if necessary.)

•**4**• Decorate the hand by making impressions with the pencil or small nail.

•**5**• Make a hole at the palm end with the hole punch or the nail, and put the yarn through. You can wear the charm or hang it.

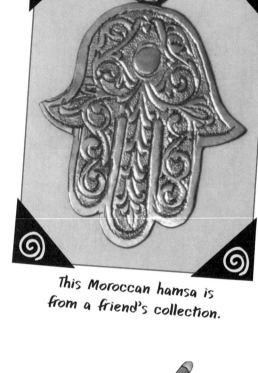

This Moroccan hamsa is from a friend's collection.

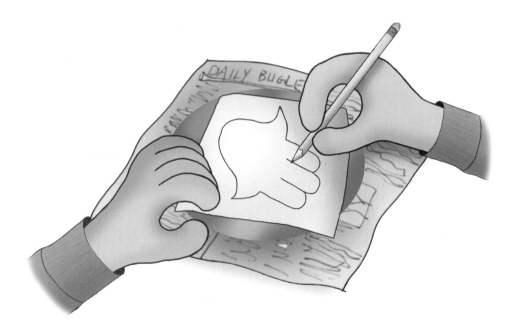

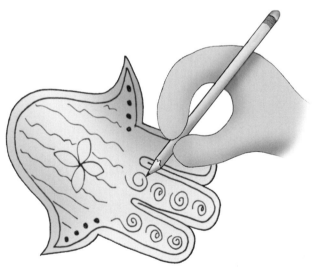

EUROPE

Although Europe is the second smallest continent, it has been a source of world-changing ideas and cultural and artistic influences for centuries. Many important inventions came from Europe, possible partly because of ideas that flowed here from other parts of the world. Explorers from Scandinavia, Spain, Portugal, Great Britain, and Italy changed world history with their travels and started a trend toward *globalization* (bringing the people of the world closer together) that continues today!

Check a more detailed map to see how close together the small countries of Europe are, and you will understand how readily cultures mix and interact here. Part of the huge country of Russia lies in Europe, with the rest reaching all the way across the continent of Asia (page 55). Eastern Russia (west of the Ural Mountains, which are shown on the map here with black triangles) is where 80 percent of the country's population lives, however, and it is considered part of eastern Europe's cultural heritage.

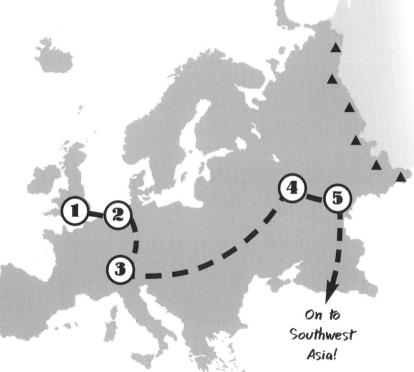

On to Southwest Asia!

In the historic city of London (1), the capital of England, you'll make an old-fashioned heart brooch to recall the Victorian era. A quick (but cold!) swim across the English Channel brings you to the Netherlands (2), to create the sickest-looking apothecary head that you can! In the beautiful Alps of Switzerland (3), you'll decorate a chain-link fence with fantastic art made of recycled clothes, just as I saw a group of Swiss schoolchildren do. We'll call it "fence art"! Now you're probably already familiar with Russian nesting dolls. But have you ever made your own? Stop in Moscow (4), the capital of Russia, to create a set! Then it's time to head east to the Volga River in Russia (5) to make a golden bowl in the world-renowed Khokhloma style.

✵ Victorian Heart Brooch

Queen Victoria, ruler of Great Britain and Ireland from 1837 to 1901, was very much in love with her husband, Prince Albert, and encouraged the romantic idea of using the language of flowers to communicate. For example, a red rose = love, a daisy = innocence, and a pansy = think of me. You'll find lots more flowers and their "meanings" at this website: <**www.victorianbazaar.com/meanings.html**>. Among the Victorians, sending flowers became a very popular way to express your feelings.

Here is a heart-shaped brooch with a little reservoir to hold water for a rosebud or other small flowers so you can use your brooch to send a special message! These pins make wonderful presents for moms and grandmas.

Great Britain and the British Empire

The term *Great Britain* refers to England, Scotland, and Wales. During Queen Victoria's reign, Great Britain developed a huge empire, with colonies in Asia, Australia, Africa, and India. At one point, Queen Victoria ruled 25% of the world's people and 30% of its land! Almost all of these colonies acquired independence after World War II.

WHAT YOU NEED

✶ 3" x 3" (7.5 x 7.5 cm) square of colored paper

✶ Scissors

✶ Pencil

✶ Flexible plastic lid at least 3" (7.5 cm) wide, clear or any color

✶ Glue gun

✶ Dried flower petals, bits of lace, narrow ribbons, small bows, tiny beads, or small pieces of cloth

✶ Pen top (from a used-up pen or marker) or empty dental-floss container with the top removed

✶ 2" (5 cm) safety pin or a pin back (from a craft store or removed from an old name badge)

WHAT YOU DO

•1• Fold the paper in half and cut out a heart-shaped pattern. Trace the heart shape onto the plastic lid. Cut it out.

•2• Glue the paper heart shape to the plastic lid. Glue the lace, flowers, and other decorations to the heart.

•3• Glue the pen top or dental-floss container upright onto the back to form a tiny vase.

•4• Glue the pin back or the safety pin onto the vase, using plenty of glue to secure it. Place it horizontally near the top of the vase as shown; if you glue it too far down, the brooch will tip forward.

•5• Put a little water in the vase and you're all ready for a tiny flower or two!

Don't Forget Your Nosegay!

During most of the Victorian era, people hadn't solved the problem of sewage in the streets. In London, it was really smelly. People would carry a little bouquet of flowers, called a *nosegay*, under their noses so they could breathe the fragrance of the blossoms as they walked through the streets!

-YOU ARE HERE-

✸ Dutch Apothecary Head

In the Netherlands (another name for Holland) in the late 1800s and early 1900s, the apothecary (ah-POTH-eh-CARE-ee) shops (the pharmacies) had wonderful wooden "signs." They were larger-than-life-size three-dimensional heads carved with sick expressions so that even people who couldn't read would know that this was a place to get medicines. The signs showed unhealthy housewives, ailing jesters, nauseated policemen, rundown royalty, and sickly sailors. They often had their tongues sticking out. Each one was quite funny and very different, but they all looked really ill.

    Make a "sick" apothecary head and put it outside the door of your room when you aren't feeling well!

WHAT YOU NEED

✻ *Papier-mâché supplies:* large bowl; 3 cups (750 ml) water; 1½ cups (375 ml) flour; wire whisk; old newspaper, torn into strips; newspaper sheets (to protect your work surface)

✻ Plastic gallon (L) jug

✻ Scissors

✻ Plastic lids, corks, egg cartons, plastic-foam peanuts, paper cups, for eyes, noses, mouths, and teeth

✻ Glue gun or wide tape

✻ Plastic container, about 5" x 8" x 2" (12.5 cm x 20 cm x 5 cm) with the lid cut off, for shoulders

✻ Acrylic paints and paintbrush

✻ Yarn, unwound cassette tapes, or Easter basket grass, for hair and mustache

✻ Cloth scraps, for hat and bandage

To make a tongue
that sticks out

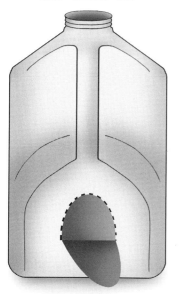

CUT ON DOTTED LINE
AND FOLD FLAP OUT

To make an
open mouth

CUT HOLE

TAPE CUP
INTO HOLE

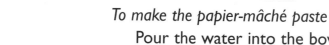

WHAT YOU DO

To make the papier-mâché paste
Pour the water into the bowl. Gradually add the flour to the water,
$1/2$ cup (125 ml) at a time and whisk it until it's smooth.

To make the head
•1• Decide if you want your jug (the basic shape your head
will be) to be right side up, upside down, with the handle in
front for a nose, or with the handle in back out of the way.

•2• Cut out or attach features to your jug to make as
sick-looking a person as you can.
Glue plastic-foam peanuts into the mouth for teeth.
Skip a few, or create a few broken ones for a great effect!
Tape or glue on crazy eyes if you want.

To use the handle as a nose

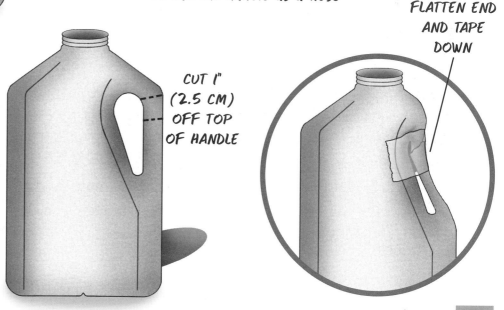

CUT 1"
(2.5 CM)
OFF TOP
OF HANDLE

FLATTEN END
AND TAPE
DOWN

A Pinch of This ...

Apothecaries made medicine for people and
for animals. They used herbs, spices, flowers,
bones, as well as strange things like spider's
legs. They mixed the active ingredients with
honey so it could be swallowed, or with fat
so it could be applied externally.

•3• Form the shoulders of your apothecary head by cutting a small, round hole in the plastic container and sticking the neck of the jug through or by gluing the bottom of the jug to the container.

•4• When you are happy with the basic shape of your apothecary head, cover all of it with several layers of papier-mâché. Remove any jewelry you're wearing, roll up your sleeves, and cover your work surface with newspaper. Smooth down each layer as you apply it. If you used a cup for the mouth, place strips of gooey newspaper in and out of the mouth so that everything is connected. Use lots of strips to connect the shoulders to the head. Let the head sit undisturbed until it's completely dry.

•5• Paint your head. When it's dry, glue on hair, a hat — or even bandages!

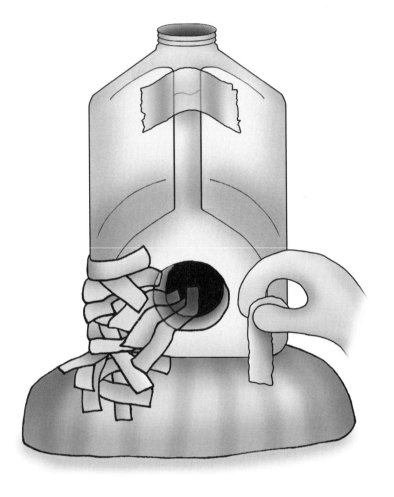

Around the World with Roberta

My son and I stayed at a youth hostel in the Netherlands, in a town called Sneek. I don't speak Dutch, but I could sort of understand some of the things people said. I was trying to read the notices on the bulletin board (all in Dutch, of course) when I saw one that seemed to be about an event for kids at a nearby museum the next day. It said "klompenbootje maken." Hmm, they were going to make (maken) something. Bootjes are boats. Klompen are the traditional Dutch wooden shoes. Were they going to make boats out of wooden shoes? I had to find out! The next day was pouring rain and hardly any kids were at the open-air folk museum, but I did get to see how they glued little sails into the wooden shoes, painted them brightly and sent them sailing off in the canals.

Swiss "Fence Art"

When my son and I were staying in Brienz, Switzerland, we learned that the local tourist bureau would let us use bicycles for free. Not wanting to miss out on that bargain, we walked into town. What they loaned out (to whomever was strong enough to use them!) were really old and very heavy Swiss Army bicycles. Once we saw the bikes we'd be riding, we were careful to plan our bicycle route through the flat glacial valley and not up the sides of the steep mountains, but it still felt as if we were biking uphill the whole time! It was, however, an absolutely beautiful route along a stream and by farms. And it was on our way back that we saw a schoolyard fence decorated with trees, horses, and mountains.

This fence art is not a traditional Swiss art style, but it deserves to become one! It sure was cool-looking! I would love to see this whimsical art beautifying chain-link fences everywhere!

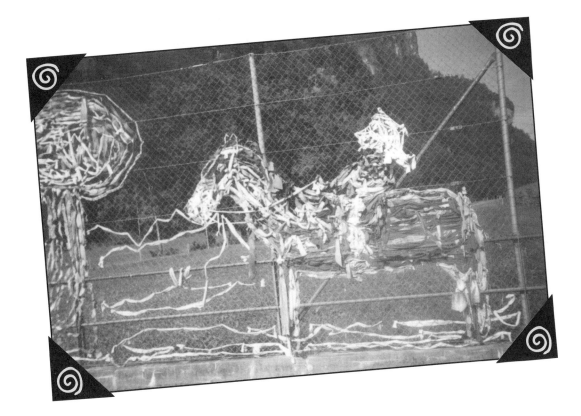

WHAT YOU NEED

✳ Old cloth or old clothes, torn into strips about 1" to 2" (2.5 to 5 cm)

✳ A chain-link fence (and permission to decorate it!)

✳ Lots of kids

WHAT YOU DO

•**1**• Plan your ideas and divide the fence into sections that will be used for each part of your scene.

•**2**• Weave the strips in and out of the chain links, each color of cloth in the proper spot. It is hard to go wrong because you can just weave more cloth over spots that need changing.

Around the World with Roberta

I drove from France to Bern, Switzerland, with my son on a very hot August day. When we got to the river Aare that surrounds Bern on three sides, we saw people bobbing in the river, floating downstream. We quickly found a place to leave the car and changed into bathing suits. We jumped into the cool, clean water and floated around all three sides of the town, enjoying marvelous views of church spires and beautiful architecture. We were happy to be cool for the first time in several days. After going under at least four bridges, we decided it was time to get out, and then realized that doing so wouldn't be easy! We saw occasional painted handrails to grab, but we missed several because the river was so swift. Then, after another bend, the current slowed down on our side of the river and we managed to grab a railing and pull ourselves out. What fun!

These California kids had a blast creating Swiss-style fence art on their school playground.

Russian Nesting Dolls

Nesting dolls are called *matryoshka* (ma-TROYSH-ka) in Russian. Traditionally, the biggest doll is a plump grandmother wearing a pretty apron with flowers and a beautiful head scarf. Inside her are many children and grandchildren. The smallest one is a baby.

The first Russian nesting doll was made in the late 1890s, and since then it has become a popular toy in Russia and around the world. Before that time, Russian artists made amazing nesting Easter eggs of wood. The idea of nesting wooden people was borrowed from Japan. Some of the modern Russian dolls have as many as 70 nesting figures! It must be hard to make that many layers that will fit together perfectly (and how big is the first one?)!

You might want to draw your family, including your pet! Ask friends and neighbors if they have any Russian nesting dolls that you can look at. Or, for inspiration, check out "Art of Matryoshka" at <**www.russiandolls.narod.ru**>, where you'll find an amazing variety of designs for inspiration, including dolls from the Museum of Russian Matryoshka in Moscow.

WHAT YOU NEED

* Scrap paper and pencil
* Plastic eggs of various sizes (try to find at least three that will nest together)
* Fine-tip permanent markers, in lots of bright colors (use only in a well-ventilated area)
* Rubbing alcohol and cotton swabs (optional)
* Section of empty egg carton

The Chinese have been making nesting boxes for at least 1,000 years. And both the Chinese and the Japanese have been making nesting people for at least 300 years. The smallest nesting doll was the size of a grain of rice, and fully decorated!

I bought these Russian matryoshka years ago for my sons when they were little.

FRONT

BACK

WHAT YOU DO

•1• Sketch some ideas for your dolls.

•2• Draw on each whole egg with permanent pens. Start with a thin black line and draw the outlines of the round face, the scarf tied in front and hanging down the back, the arms at the sides, and the apron in front.

•3• Fill in with colors to create a beautiful doll. Work carefully, as permanent-marker ink will smudge if you rub it before it dries.

If you don't like what you drew, you can quickly rub it away. Or, if you change your mind after the ink dries, remove it with a cotton swab dipped in rubbing alcohol. Allow the spot to dry before drawing again. Set the finished dolls in a section of egg carton to dry.

Golden Khokhloma Bowl

The people of Khokhloma (HOK-la-ma), a village in Russia on the Volga River, have been making beautiful wooden bowls, cups, and spoons for more than 300 years. Rather than chopping down their aspen and birch forests to make farmland, they decided to use some of the trees to make useful items to trade for food. They soon discovered a beautiful way to create a gold color on carved wood by baking it with a layer of powdered tin (nowadays aluminum is used) at a high heat. They used this technique to create the golden insides of the carved items. To decorate the outsides, they were inspired by the plants they saw around them: the ripe red strawberries, the blossoming fruit trees, and the variously shaped leaves. They created such beautiful carved items that people all over Russia traded with them and the town became prosperous. This style of decoration became known as Khokhloma painting.

You can use papier-mâché and acrylic paints to make a bowl inspired by this beautiful Russian tradition.

WHAT YOU NEED

* *Papier-mâché supplies:* large bowl; 3 cups (750 ml) water; 1½ cups (375 ml) flour; wire whisk; old newspaper, torn into strips; newspaper sheets (to protect your work surface)
* Shallow bowl with a smooth bottom to use as a mold (The shape of the *outside* of the bottom of the mold will be the shape of the *inside* of your homemade bowl.)
* Plastic wrap
* Tape
* Cake rack
* Scissors
* Shiny fabric paints or acrylics: gold (iridescent is pretty), black, red, and green
* Paintbrushes, one small and one medium sized

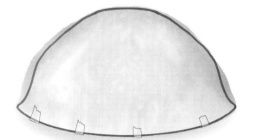

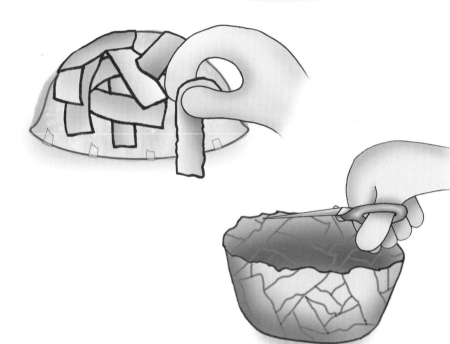

WHAT YOU DO

To make the papier-mâché paste

Pour the water into the large bowl. Gradually add the flour to the water, ½ cup (125 ml) at a time and whisk it until it's smooth.

To make the bowl

•**1**• Place the bowl upside down on your work surface. Cover the bottom of the bowl mold with plastic wrap and tape it to the inside.

•**2**• Remove any jewelry you're wearing and roll up your sleeves. Cover your work surface with newspaper. Dip the newspaper strips in the papier-mâché paste and layer them on the bottom of the bowl mold. Be sure to crisscross them to completely cover the surface. Make four to eight complete layers, smoothing down each layer.

•**3**• Slip the wet papier-mâché shape off the bowl carefully so it doesn't squish, and remove the plastic layer. Dry it in the sun on a cake rack. Turn it over when it is mostly dry so the bottom will dry. This may take only a few hours if the day is warm.

•**4**• Use scissors to trim the edge of the bowl to make a smooth, even rim.

•**5**• Paint the inside of the bowl with gold paint. Let it dry.

•**6**• Paint the outside of the bowl with black paint. Let it dry.

•**7**• Paint a pretty pattern in red, gold, and green on the outside of your bowl. Use the small brush so you can make small intricate designs. Traditional Russian designs are flowers and plants: red berries, golden leaves, blossoming branches, and green tendrils.

•**8**• Let your bowl dry and use it to store your treasures. Just don't use it for storing or serving food (sorry!).

ASIA

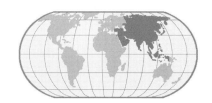

Asia just might set the record for notable achievements, that's for sure! The world's largest continent, it has the country with the biggest population (China) *and* the second biggest population (India). It has the tallest mountain (Everest), as well as the country with the most number of islands (that's Indonesia, with a whopping 13,677!). It's the only continent that crosses both the Arctic Circle and the equator! Asia is where some of the world's oldest civilizations arose and where many of the world's popular religions began. It is a culturally rich and diverse place, where ancient traditions collide with modern lifestyles every day.

On your first stop, you'll try your hand at the ancient Persian craft of rug-making (1). In Rajasthan in western India (2), you'll make a wedding bag (that will someday be filled with money!). Now, I hope you're ready to celebrate the New Year! You'll trek way up into the Himalayas to learn a traditional custom from Nepal (3) for this holiday. As you travel through China (4), let your imagination soar as you create traditional hats and shoes the kids there wear to protect them from evil spirits. Then you'll hike the hilly country of Laos (5) to celebrate the New Year again with the Iu Mien people. Then it's on to Japan (6) for one last New Year's celebration! Make a traditional wish doll and don't forget to make a wish while you paint in one eye! Then your handmade *koi-nobori,* a Japanese windsock, will show you the way that the wind is blowing as you get ready to sail down through the South China Sea. You'll end your Asian tour on the Indonesian island of Java (7), where you'll use the ancient dyeing technique of batik.

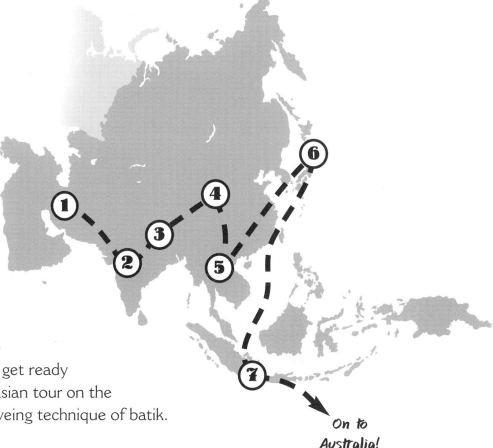

On to Australia!

✳ Persian (Mini) Rug

Beautiful intricate Persian rugs were originally made as floor coverings for tents to keep people's feet warm. The rugs are made of knotted wool on a cotton background. The wool is dyed with insects, roots, and bark. Red and black are two of the most traditional colors for a Persian rug, but others are used as well. The designs are of animals, birds, flowers, fruits, and geometric shapes.

It's hard to know how long people in the Middle East have been making rugs, because most of the rugs rotted, but the oldest rug that has been preserved is from 500 B.C. Even today, people in the Middle East are making these beautiful rugs by hand and selling them all around the world.

Make yourself a knotted mini Persian rug and enjoy the soft feel of it. It makes a comfy wrist rest when you're using the computer! And remember, a handmade rug is never perfect. There is a Persian saying that a rug should be "perfectly imperfect and precisely imprecise." So just enjoy making and using yours!

500 B.C.?

500 B.C. was about 2,500 years ago! The counting of time in the Western world dates from the early days of Christianity. The year "1" stands for the year that Christians believe Jesus Christ was born. Anytime before that is called B.C. (before Christ). Anytime after (the time we're in now) is A.D., (*anno Domini,* Latin for "in the year of the Lord").

WHAT YOU NEED

* Masking or clear tape
* Latch hook canvas, about 6" x 6" (15 x 15 cm) with 3 or 4 holes per inch (2.5 cm), available from a craft store
* Colored pens and paper (optional)
* Latch hook
* Yarn cut in 2½" or 3" (6 or 7.5 cm) pieces (you can buy it precut for rug-making)
* Yarn, 2 yards (2 m) long
* Yarn needle
* Scissors

WHAT YOU DO

•**1**• Tape the edges of the canvas so it doesn't unravel while you're making the rug. You should cover two rows on each edge.

•**2**• You can plan your design on paper and sketch it onto the rug backing, or you can just make up your pattern as you go.

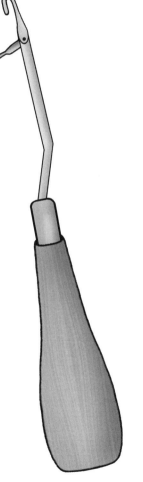

LATCH HOOK

Where *Is* Persia?

If you look for Persia on a modern map, you won't find it. A culturally rich center of art and architecture since ancient times, Persia was renamed Iran in 1935. You've probably heard of the Persian Gulf, which borders Iran, Iraq, Kuwait, Saudia Arabia, and other Arab nations. It is a major shipping and oil supply route for this region.

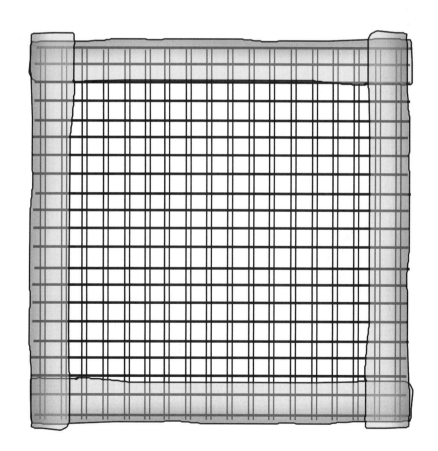

•3• To "hook" the design, use the latch hook to knot the short yarn pieces on the canvas as shown.

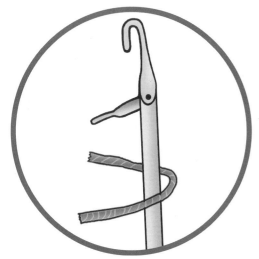

a) Put a short piece of yarn around the tool.

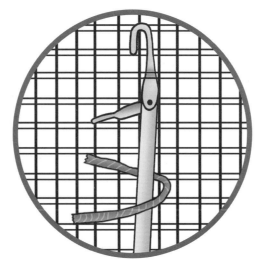

b) Push the point end of the tool through a hole in the canvas and back out the next hole.

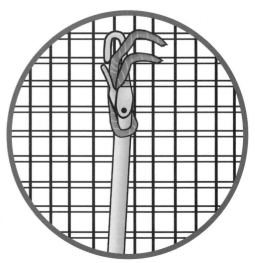

c) Put the two ends of the yarn across the open hook.

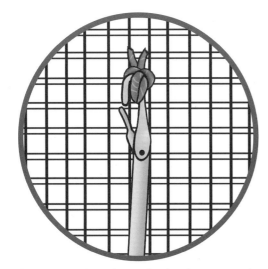

d) Pull the tool back through the holes in the canvas and through the loop of yarn that's around the tool, making sure that the hook catches both yarn ends.

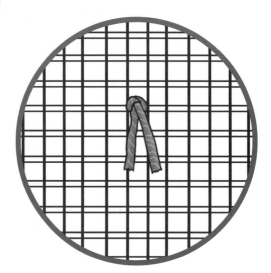

e) Keep pulling the tool so it comes out, creating a knot.

•4• Continue adding knots of different-colored yarn until your pattern is complete.

•5• Gently pull off the tape. Single-thread (page 118) the yarn on the yarn needle and knot the yarn. Fold the edge of the canvas to the back and whipstitch (page 118) it to the back of the rug.

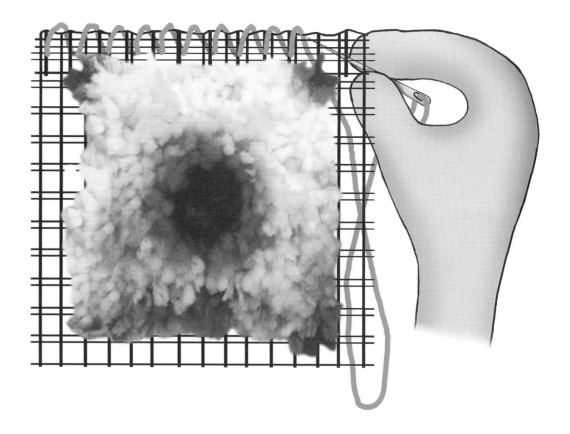

Crafty Idea! Give your rug a haircut! You can trim the yarn a little to make the rug more three-dimensional. For example, trim the center of a flower and leave the petals of the flower longer. Trim the background yarn to a shorter length so the flower pattern stands out.

Around the World with Roberta

As soon as I stepped off the train in Istanbul, Turkey, I knew I had arrived in the Middle East. First there was the sound of the music, with its distinctive rhythms, playing everywhere day and night. Then I looked up and saw the tall minarets and rounded domes of the magnificent mosques. Even though they are sacred, I was allowed to look into the Hagia Sophia (a huge cathedral) and the Mosque of Sultan Ahmed (known as "the Blue Mosque" because of its gorgeous blue tiles) and see the huge domed rooms. I had never been in such lovely spaces! And then I looked at the floor — it was a thickly layered sea of amazing carpets, each more beautiful than the one before.

✴ Rajasthani Wedding Bag from India

The state of Rajasthan (RA-ja-stan) in northwestern India is known for its handcrafts. One example is the beautiful purses the brides there use to hold the coins and jewels they receive at their weddings. The purse, usually handmade by the bride's grandmother, is made of fancy cloth decorated with gold threads, tiny mirrors, beads, and sequins. What is really fun about this bag is the way you fold the square piece of cloth to makes a square purse, just like an envelope. Use it to hold your favorite jewelry, special coins, or other treasures!

WHAT YOU NEED

✴ Square piece of cloth, from about 6" to 10" (15 to 25 cm)*

✴ Ruler

✴ Scissors

✴ Sewing machine (optional)

✴ Embroidery needle and embroidery floss

✴ Embroidery hoop, any size (optional)

✴ Sequins

✴ Beads with holes big enough for an embroidery needle to fit through (optional)

✴ Large button

✴ Chalk

*Pieces of upholstery cloth are perfect, and some upholstery stores give away their old sample books.

Meet Rajasthan

India's second-largest state, Rajasthan, is just a little bit smaller than Montana. Located in the northwest corner of the country, it borders Pakistan. Rajasthan has areas of dry desert climate with camels, but also has swamps with crocodiles and forests with tigers and bears.

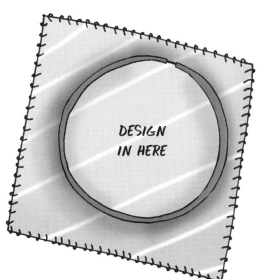

DESIGN
IN HERE

•1• Ask an adult to help you measure and trim your cloth so it's a perfect square. Stitch the edges so they don't fray. You can use a hemstitch on the sewing machine or a whipstitch (page 118) using the embroidery needle and floss to give a fancy decorative edge.

•2• Put the embroidery hoop on your cloth to hold it tight, if you want. The hoop will keep your stitching in the center of the cloth (you don't want to sew on the four corners because they are where you will fold the cloth).

•3• Single-thread the needle (page 118) and knot the end. Pull the needle through the cloth so that the knot is on the wrong side of the fabric (the side that will face in); thread a few sequins and beads onto the needle. Push the needle back down through the cloth to hold them in place.

Continue until you have all the decorations you want. Snip the thread and knot it.

A Traditional Indian Wedding

Following the age-old custom, the bride and groom in India are chosen for each other by their families. The ceremony takes place at the bride's home. Her family and friends spend the hours preceding the wedding lavishing attention on her and helping make her especially beautiful. The groom arrives on a white horse and meets his bride, sometimes for the first time! The ceremony takes place under a canopied altar called a *mandapam* right in the middle of a noisy crowd of celebrating family and friends. During the party that follows, the guests give money and jewelry to the bride to help her in her married life.

•4• Place your square with the decorated side facing *down* and fold three corners to the middle as shown.

•5• Rethread the needle with embroidery floss and knot it. Use the backstitch (page 116) to sew the edges of the cloth together where they meet. It takes only two short seams to form the bag!

Keep your stitches loose enough so the seam lies flat. Be careful not to sew through the front of the bag as you stitch into the corners.

•6• Sew the button (page 117) on the front just below where the points meet. (You don't want your jewels to fall out!)

•7• Lay the top flap of the bag over the button and mark with chalk the position of the button underneath. Cut a slit for the buttonhole and whipstitch (page 118) around it.

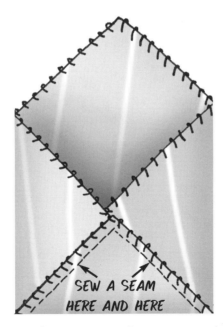

SEW A SEAM HERE AND HERE

Fold the sides in, then fold up the bottom corner so the edges overlap.

CUT HERE

Marigold Necklace for the Nepali New Year

Nepal is a tiny mountainous country tucked between India and China. The Nepali and Indian Hindus celebrate the New Year with a five-day celebration called Tihar, the festival of lights, honoring Laxmi, or Lakshmi (LAK-shmee), the goddess of wealth. One of the traditions involves making garlands from marigold blossoms to honor certain animals. People decorate their homes with these garlands and give them as gifts.

Make a bright-colored garland to celebrate the New Year or to give as a gift to someone you appreciate the whole year through — your brother or sister, your pet, or maybe even your cow! The traditional garlands are made with fresh marigolds, but you can also use daisies or other flowers that grow abundantly where you live; just ask permission before you pick. If you can't find any fresh flowers, you can use dried flowers from a craft store — the brightest yellow or orange you can find!

WHAT YOU NEED

* Strong thread, 6' (1.8 m)
* Needle
* Scissors
* Marigolds or other flowers

Traveling the Trade Route

When the Chinese officially took over Tibet in 1965, many Tibetans left their beloved country to look for a better life over the border in Nepal or India. On my hike up the Kali Gandaki River in 1971, I met many Tibetan people hiking out of that deep river gorge, which forms a natural trail through the extremely high range of mountains called the Himalayas. This trail has been used for trade between Nepal and Tibet for a long time. Long ago, rice from India was traded for salt from Tibet. Now caravans of small donkeys carry everything from lamp kerosene and socks to soup and cookies up into the high country, and bring animal hides and salt back out. At higher elevations, supplies are carried by a stronger animal that is a cross between a yak and a cow. Called *dzo* (male) and *dzomo* (female), they are sturdy and short with long horns and a thick tail.

WHAT YOU DO

•1• Double-thread the needle (page 116) and tie a strong knot.

•2• Snip a blossom so it has about a ½" (1 cm) stem. Push the needle through the hollow stem and up through the center of the flower.

•3• Push the flower to the bottom of the thread up against the knot. Continue snipping and stringing the blossoms until your thread is full.

•4• Tie the ends together to make a garland and decorate the animal (or sibling) of your choice! The necklaces are very pretty fresh, and also look nice when the blossoms dry.

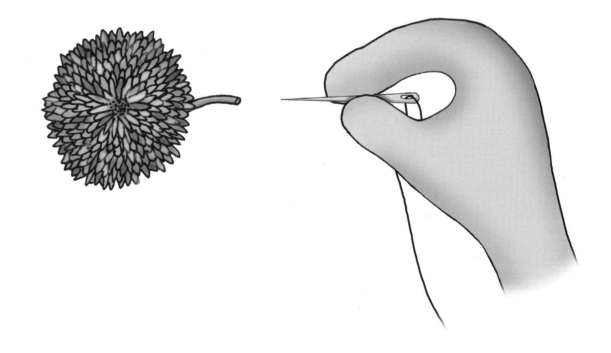

The Festival of Lights

Tihar starts on the 13th day of the waning moon in October. During the festival, crows are fed to bring good luck to the people. Dogs are honored and thanked for their work as guardians of the house. They are garlanded with marigold necklaces and given especially tasty food to eat. Cows are also honored with garlands and good food. Following Hindu belief, cows are the most sacred animal. The cows are very happy with their necklaces and like to eat them right up!

People decorate their houses with flowers and garlands. They perform traditional rituals, then gather together to play gambling games. On the last day, brothers and sisters honor each other, exchanging gifts and blessings.

Around the World with Roberta

In the spring of 1971, I went trekking in Nepal. I backpacked up into the high mountains going from village to village, crossing rushing river gorges between glaciated mountains. In the evening I would find a family who would feed me and let me sleep on grass mats on the floor of their home. They served popcorn for breakfast, and rice, curried lentils, potatoes, and a leafy green vegetable for dinner. I later learned that it was stinging nettles!

One day it started to hail fast. As I ducked into a nearby public shelter, I saw four piles of greens hurrying up the hill toward me. When they came into the little hut I saw that they were young girls carrying huge baskets of nettles. We exchanged smiles but I shrank out of the way of the stinging nettles. Evidently once nettles are cooked, they no longer sting and they taste good. I have always wondered how the girls gathered them without getting hurt!

I met this Nepali girl with her basket of greens on a trail heading toward Annapurna, a group of towering Himalayan peaks. She was a little shy but very friendly and happy to pose for a picture!

Asia **65**

✺ Chinese Children's Hat

Traditionally, young Chinese children wear beautiful colorful hats. A child's mother or grandmother hand-sews and embroiders the hat to look like a tiger, elephant, pig, dragon, panther, dog, or fish. These animals have lucky qualities that protect the child. For extra protection, some hats have two tigers, one on top of the other. Lion hats are the strongest protection of all and are made only for a child who needs extra care. These hats also have decorations that are just plain fun — like puffy balls on springs that bounce as the kid walks.

You can make a Chinese hat to surprise and amuse your friends!

WHAT YOU NEED

* ✳ Bright-colored cap, with the bill cut off
* ✳ Colorful pieces of felt or fabric scraps
* ✳ Egg cartons
* ✳ Acrylic paint and paintbrush (optional)
* ✳ Scissors
* ✳ Glue gun
* ✳ Gold or shiny ribbons, colorful yarns, tassels, pom-poms, old shoulder pads (removed from an old blouse or shirt), pipe cleaners, gold foil, sections of old fringe, beads, bells, for decorations
* ✳ 1" to 2" (2.5 to 5 cm) springs
* ✳ Embroidery needle and embroidery floss
* ✳ Permanent markers

WHAT YOU DO

•1• Think of what animal you want to represent and chose your materials accordingly.

•2• Use your imagination to decorate the cap with eyes and ears, tongue and teeth, whiskers and fur, tail and claws. Single egg-carton cups (painted or covered with fabric) make great bulgy eyes. To make ears, cut a single egg cup in half and line it with fabric or felt. Or, glue on the shoulder pads for nice big ears!

•3• Some hats have little bells to scare off evil spirits. Or, make a pom-pom as shown. Tie the pom-pom to the end of a spring. Glue the spring to the hat as shown on the finished hat (page 68).

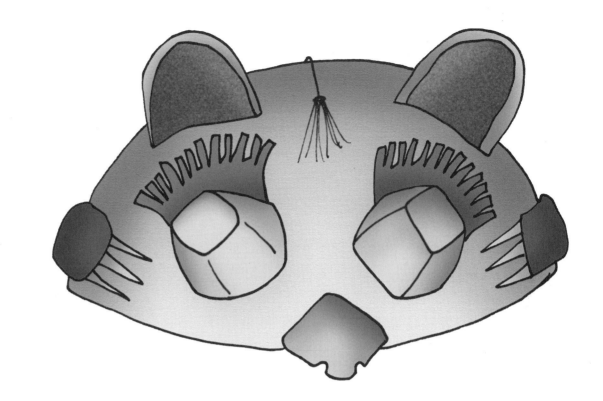

Wrap thin yarn around your fingers 50 to 100 times.

TIE

CUT

Slip the yarn off your fingers.

•4• Most traditional Chinese children's hats have something trailing down the back, so you may want to make a tail flap. You can sew on a piece of cloth, using the whipstitch (page 118). Or, make a fringe: Thread the needle with embroidery floss and sew in and out along the back of the cap as shown. You can make the fringe any length you like.

When you are finished sewing, knot the thread. Snip along the bottom of the threads to create a fringe as shown.

•5• You can also make the tail of the animal stick up behind the hat, using several pipe cleaners twisted together or a pipe cleaner wrapped in cloth and bent into a tail shape.

•SINCE LONG AGO•

Like parents everywhere, Chinese parents want to ensure their children will live long and healthy lives. Particularly in the rural villages, it has long been the tradition to make clothing in the shapes of animals, like a dog or a pig, as a way of warding off evil spirits. The superstition was that if the clothing could disguise the child as one of those animals, the spirits would have no reason to harm him. The clothing was also decorated with special symbols. A bat is a good luck symbol, for example, because the Chinese word for happiness is pronounced the same as the word for bat (*fu*). Rats, fish, butterflies, watermelons, and lotus blossoms are other good luck symbols.

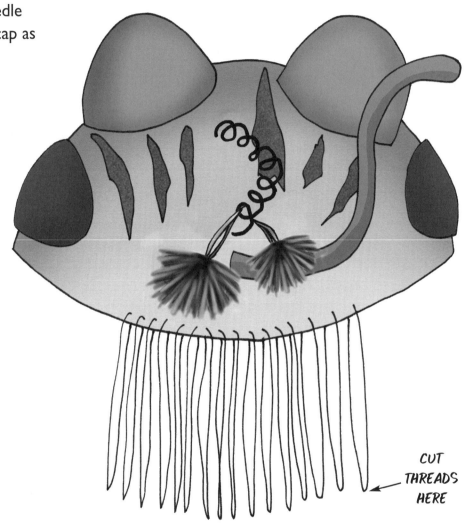

CUT THREADS HERE

Chinese Tiger Shoes

In the old days in China, children weren't given a name until they were one month old. On this day a child got his first haircut, and was given his first protective hat (page 66). The family and friends would have a big celebration with lots of food and presents. The baby would also be given his first pair of tiger shoes, handmade of silk cloth and beautifully embroidered. The tigers on the shoes have their eyes wide open to protect the child and keep him from tripping when he learns to walk!

You can make this cozy slipper version look like tigers or your favorite animal.

WHAT YOU NEED

* Shoes that fit you well (not too much bigger than your feet)
* Marker
* Scissors
* Piece of rug pad (the strong quilted type is perfect), from a carpet/rug store
* Old pair of your socks, 2 pieces of fuzzy cloth (about 5" x 7"/12.5 x 17.5 cm), or 2 shoulder pads (removed from an old shirt or blouse)
* Glue gun
* Thin but strong cloth ribbon, 2 pieces about 10" (25 cm) long
* Buttons, beads, wiggly eyes, pipe cleaners, cloth scraps, pom-poms

WHAT YOU DO

•1• Trace around the shoes onto the rug pad. Cut out both soles.

•2• To make the toe caps from your socks, cut them off at the heel, or about 5" (12.5 cm) from the toe. Slip them over the ends of the rug-pad soles.

   If using cloth or shoulder pads for the toe caps, glue around the edges of the toe caps (don't glue the straight edge or you won't be able to put the shoe on). Press the edges onto the sole.

•3• Glue the ribbon over the toe cap and around the sole to help hold the shoe together.

•4• Now comes the fun part — making the slippers look like animals. You can glue on wide eyes and perky ears. You can make the nose so it wiggles when you wiggle your toes. Add a mouth, and make your slippers "talk" when you curl your toes. How about whiskers that stick out or tails that drag behind your slippers? If you made a mouse, see if you can get your foam soles to squeak as you walk! If you make a dog, you can add a "leash" that ties around your ankle!

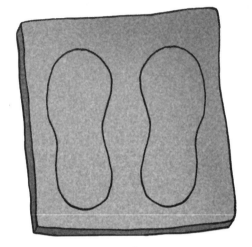

•SINCE LONG AGO•

Tigers have been an important symbol in China for at least 6,000 years. We know this because of the recent discovery of a tiger and a dragon made of shells, found in an ancient grave.

   The tiger was used for protection on clothing because it was believed this fierce beast would scare away ghosts. The character for the word tiger and the character for wealth are both pronounced *hu* so parents hoped tiger clothing would help their child grow up to be wealthy as well as brave!

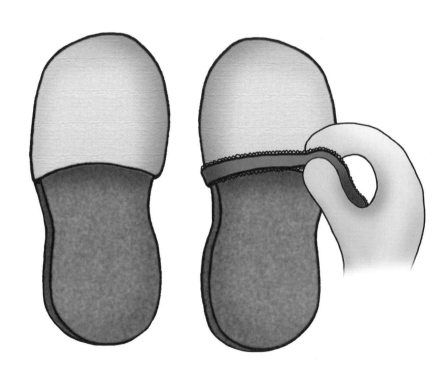

The Kids' Multicultural Craft Book

Iu Mien Egg Holder

The Iu Mien (YOU myen) people live in the hill country of the northern parts of Laos, Vietnam, and Myanmar (formerly Burma) in southeast Asia. They celebrate their New Year in early February with housecleaning and feasting. People dye eggs red and wear them around their necks in a special knotted string to bring good luck. Their celebration has a similarity to a February holiday that you know about — Valentine's Day! New Year is the time that the Iu Mien young people try to meet their future spouses. Young people who have fallen in love give each other these red eggs.

Here is an easy-to-make yarn egg holder that will bring you good luck, Iu Mien style!

Try speaking Mienh!

The Iu Mien people have an interesting melodious language. For instance, if you say the word *mai* with different rising, falling, and or flat tones, it can mean "to buy," "to sell," "to have," or "not." It also means "teak tree" and "lopsided"! It would be important to say that word correctly!

To hear some spoken words in the Mienh language and learn some phrases, check out this website, <**www.mienh.net/language/language.html**>. It also has information about Iu Mien history and culture, and a photo album of Iu Mien people from different regions of Asia.

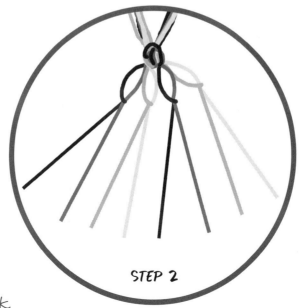

STEP 1

WHAT YOU NEED

✳ Yarn in different colors, 4 pieces, each 54" (135 cm) long

✳ Hardboiled eggs dyed red with egg dyes or food coloring

WHAT YOU DO

•1• Line up the four pieces of yarn, fold them in half (so they're doubled), and tie all eight ends together loosely about 8" (20 cm) from the bottom.

•2• Using small double knots (page 116), tie two of the strand ends together 2" (5 cm) below the big loose knot you just made. Repeat with other strands to form a total of four knots.

8" (20 cm)

STEP 2

The Iu Mien on the Move

Many Iu Mien in Laos escaped from the terror of the Pathet Lao Communist government in the mid-1970s, fleeing to refugee camps along the border of Thailand. Families made the dangerous journey on foot across rough terrain (often traveling at night to avoid soldiers) and then crossed the mighty Mekong River that separates Laos and Thailand. Although the refugees were safe in the camps, the living conditions were very difficult.

From there, many Iu Mien began immigrating to the United States. The first arrived in 1980 and since then an estimated 20,000 Iu Mien immigrants have resettled in America, many in California. Maintaining traditions and crafts from their rural lifestyle of the past is one way the Iu Mien have preserved their cultural identity in a new, very different, country.

•3• Working with one knot at a time, separate the strands just below the knot to join one strand from one knot with one strand from the next knot over; knot them together about 1" (2.5 cm) below the last row of knots.

Continue joining adjacent strands for a total of four knots to form a net.

•4• Separate the strands again and tie four more knots 1" (2.5 cm).

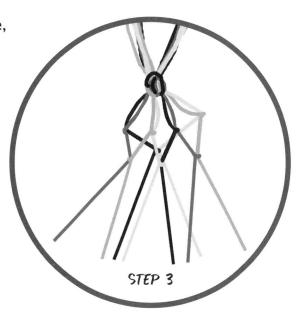

STEP 3

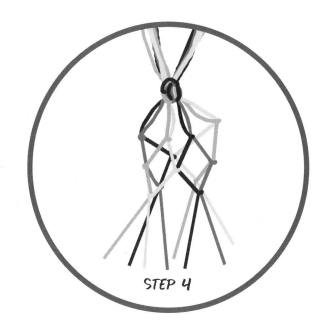

STEP 4

All You Need Are ... Rubber Bands!

The Iu Mien kids in the Thai refugee camps amused themselves creatively with rubber bands. They made chains of them and tied them in a circle about 6' (1.8 m) around. Two kids would hold the elastic loop while a third one jumped higher and higher, performing complicated foot movements. It took practice to get good. Can you guess the game? Hint: It's also popular in America. If you said Chinese jump rope, you're right!

Once while I was waiting for a train in Thailand, I saw a group of boys intently playing a game I had never seen. They needed only rubber bands to play. They would get down close to the ground and blow on a rubber band lying in the dirt. If they could get it to jump up onto another person's rubber band, they would get to keep both bands. The boys would display the bands they had won on their wrists — some had quite a few!

•5• Tie all eight ends together about 1" (2.5 cm) below the last row of knots. You should have 1" to 2" (2.5 to 5 cm) of yarn left hanging free.

•6• Loosen the first big knot so you can slip the egg into the net basket. Tighten that knot so it holds the egg snugly in place.

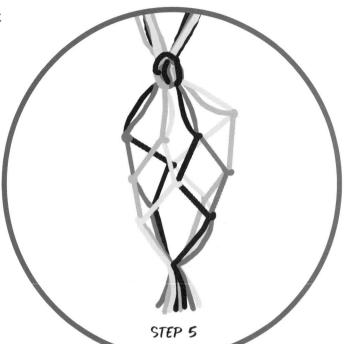

STEP 5

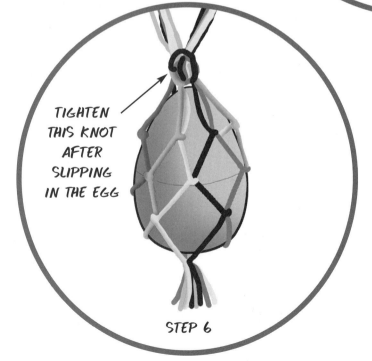

TIGHTEN THIS KNOT AFTER SLIPPING IN THE EGG

STEP 6

More Tiger Luck!

Just as with the Chinese (page 66), the tiger is a symbol of good luck to the Iu Mien. The third day after New Year's is called Tiger Sleeping Day. To bring good luck, everyone stays in the village and keeps very quiet. The next day is Tiger Walking Day and people can talk again, but they still can't go out to the fields to tend their gardens.

Around the World with Roberta

When I traveled in the northern part of Thailand, I took an all-day ride on a dilapidated bus to Chiang Rai. We passed lumbering operations where elephants were being used to move logs! When we arrived in Chiang Rai, we were very, very hungry, but there seemed to be only one small restaurant, serving one dish — the spiciest soup I've ever eaten. I couldn't tell exactly what was in the soup, but it sure looked like bugs! We were happy to find food, and it gave us the energy to hike way up into the hills to visit several villages.

Daruma, or Japanese Wish Doll

In Japan, welcoming the New Year is the most important celebration of the year. Crowds of people visit the ancient Shinto shrines or Buddhist temples to pray for good luck for the coming year. Most people dress their children up in beautiful *kimonos* (the long robes with wide sleeves and sashes), and many adults also dress up in fancy traditional clothing. At the shrine, they buy *daruma* (dah-roo-ma) wish dolls as well as bamboo arrows, called *hamaya* (ha-mah-yah), which are taken home and kept for the next year to keep bad luck away from the family.

Many Japanese people also make a papier-mâché *daruma* doll each New Year so that they can make a wish. As they paint the iris of one eye they make a wish. They paint in the other eye when the wish comes true!

WHAT YOU NEED

* *Papier-mâché supplies:* large bowl; 3 cups (750 ml) water; 1½ cups (375 ml) flour; wire whisk; tan or white construction paper torn in small pieces; newspaper sheets (to protect your work surface)

* Plastic egg that opens

* Glue gun or modeling clay

* Pennies, glass marbles, or metal washers for weights

* Pencil

* Acrylic paints in white, red, black, and yellow

* Paintbrushes

* Small paper cup (optional)

* Fabric paint in tubes

Roll with the Punches!

These dolls are designed so they will right themselves when knocked over. Japanese parents give them to their children to teach them the value of not giving up. Have you heard the phrase "roll with the punches"? It means when you're disappointed or when something bad happens unexpectedly, rather than dwell on it, you pick yourself up and try again. You've probably had adults tell you not to give up even when something is hard. In Japan, kids hear the same thing from their parents!

To make the papier-mâché paste
Pour the water into the bowl. Gradually add the flour to the water, ½ cup (125 ml) at a time and whisk it until it's smooth.

To make the egg

•**1**• Open the egg and glue or stick with clay the weights into the less pointed end of the egg. Try to center the weight in the bottom.

•**2**• Put the top of the egg back on and set the egg on a level surface. See if it will right itself when you push the top gently. Add more weight or reposition the weights if necessary until it does.

•**3**• Remove any jewelry you're wearing and roll up your sleeves. Cover your work surface with newspaper. Dip the paper strips in the papier-mâché paste and wrap them around the egg. As you cover the egg, try to add more layers to the bottom so it is even wider on the bottom than the egg shape. Be sure to keep the bottom rounded so it will still bobble back and forth!

•**4**• Let the covered egg dry in the sun. It will take a few hours or a day, depending on how thick you made the papier-mâché.

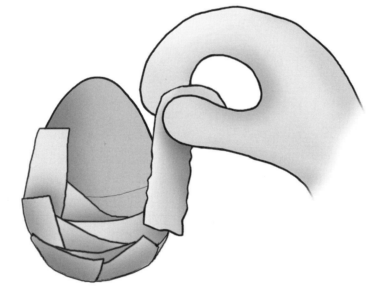

To paint the face

•**1**• Look at the illustrations for examples of traditional faces. Try out your design ideas by drawing with pencil first. Be sure to make the face large so you have plenty of space for the features, especially the large eyes.

•**2**• Paint the face area white; let it dry. Paint the rest of the doll red. You can put it in a small cup to hold it while you paint the back, top, and bottom. Let it dry.

•**3**• Paint black features for the face with a fine brush or with fabric paint. Don't forget to make a wish as you paint one of the pupils. Let it dry.

•**4**• Paint in yellow shapes over the dried red paint to finish your traditional design; let it dry. Don't forget to paint the other eye when the wish comes true!

Mochi pounding

Another favorite New Year's event in Japan is mochi pounding. Sweet rice is cooked until it's gluey and then dumped into a big wooden mortar where it is pounded hard with big mallets. Two or three people work at once, alternating so quickly that they almost collide. The pounding is accompanied by drumming and chanting. It looks almost like a vigorous dance and lasts for about an hour. In the end the rice becomes an unbelievably rubbery paste, called *mochi.* It is good luck to eat some, but be sure to take very tiny bites because it will be like swallowing a piece of gum!

If you live near an Asian cultural center, you might be lucky enough to see a *mochitsuki* (mochi pounding ceremony) — it is quite wonderful to watch! Or, check out photos of this ritual at **<www.calacademy.org/research/anthropology/tap/archive/ 2000/2000-05--mochi.html>**.

✹ Koi-nobori, or Japanese Wind-Sock Fish

May 5th is Children's Day in Japan. On that day Japanese families hang carp wind socks on tall bamboo poles. They are made of paper or cloth and painted red and blue like the colorful carp fish. The Japanese respect that particular fish because it swims against the current and leaps up waterfalls like a salmon. Japanese parents want their children to be strong and never give up, just like the carp. On this special day, a fish is flown for each child, with larger ones for the larger kids.

Celebrate Children's Day where you live, or another special day like your birthday, by making and flying a colorful Japanese wind sock.

WHAT YOU NEED

* Old newspaper
* Sleeve from an old long-sleeved shirt, white or other pale color (be sure to get permission before you cut off the sleeve!)
* Fabric paints, or acrylic paints and paintbrushes (blue, red, and gold are traditional colors and glittery paints look especially nice, but you can be creative!), or felt-tip markers (EASY NO-MESS FISH, page 79)
* Gallon size (L) round plastic bottle
* String or yarn, three 3' (1 m) pieces
* Scissors or knife (for use with adult help)
* Hole punch
* Glue gun or stapler

WHAT YOU DO

•**1**• Fold a section of newspaper and insert it into the sleeve. Cover your work surface with newspaper (and you might want to put on old shirt).

•**2**• Paint the front of the sleeve. Remember that the shoulder end will be the mouth of the fish so make a big eye at that end. Leave 1" to 2" (2.5 to 5 cm) unpainted at the mouth end for folding over. Then paint a lot of glittery scales down to the cuff end where you can paint the tail fins. Let the paint dry, then turn it over and paint the other side.

•**3**• Cut a 1" to 2" (2.5 to 5 cm) wide band out of the plastic bottle. Use scissors or a knife, depending on how stiff your bottle is. Make small holes in the band on three sides, using a hole punch.

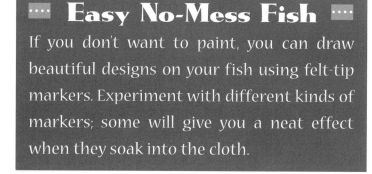

Easy No-Mess Fish

If you don't want to paint, you can draw beautiful designs on your fish using felt-tip markers. Experiment with different kinds of markers; some will give you a neat effect when they soak into the cloth.

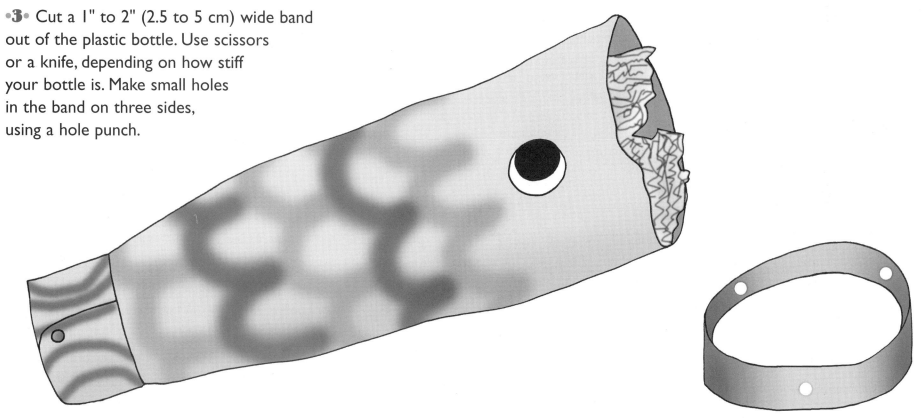

•4• Fold the mouth end of the fish over the edge of the band and glue or staple it in place. Snip tiny holes in the cloth to line up with the holes in the band. String the yarn through the holes and tie it.

•5• Run around and make your fish fly. With adult help, you can attach it to a tall pole and watch the fish "swim" in the air.

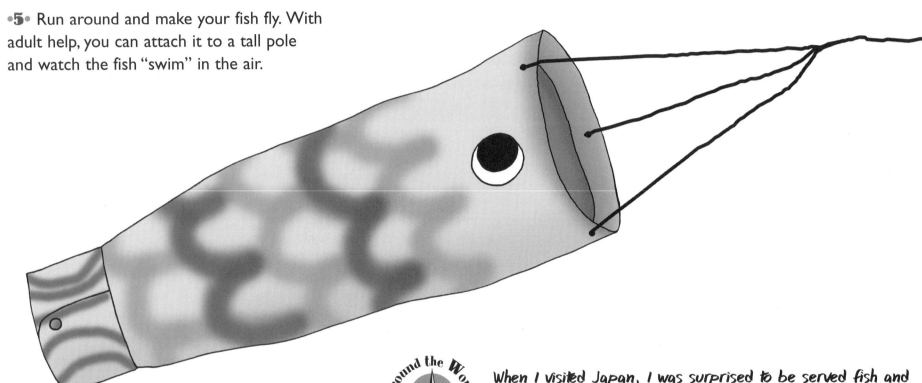

Around the World with Roberta

When I visited Japan, I was surprised to be served fish and soup for breakfast. I had to learn to eat the little bony fish with chopsticks and slurp the soup. When you eat soup in Japan, you hold the bowl up near your face and use your chopsticks to pick up any chunks. Then you drink the soup. It makes a nice slurping sound because you are drinking a hot liquid out of a bowl. It's not considered the least bit impolite to do this. I've never understood why we Americans consider it impolite to slurp. When I'm drinking a milk shake with a straw, I always want to get the last drops, even if it makes a loud noise!

Javanese Batik Handkerchief

On Java, one of the many islands that makes up Indonesia, beautiful intricate patterns called *batik* are made on cloth using wax and dyes. Women apply the wax with a *canting* (TJAN-ting), a special tool with a very tiny hole so that the hot wax can be applied in very thin lines and tiny dots. You'll use a much easier method (a paintbrush) and will apply wax in large areas that you can crack the wax and create interesting patterns. Batik designs are unique because the wax cracks in a different way on each piece of fabric.

You will need an adult helper for this project; you have to be very careful when working with hot wax, as well as with the dye, which can stain things.

Crafty Idea! You can use old candle stubs and crayons to make colorful wax. Just melt them down following the instructions in step 1, page 82, melting each color in a separate can.

WHAT YOU NEED

* *To create the wax patterns:* beeswax or paraffin; small tin can; food-warming tray or an old pot, a stove, and an adult helper; small inexpensive paintbrush

* A piece of 100% cotton cloth (well-washed handkerchiefs, place mats, cloth napkins, or sheets work well)

* *To dye the cloth:* package or bottle of *cold*-water dye (using hot water will melt the wax and destroy your pattern!), plastic dye pot, rubber gloves, and an adult helper

* Iron, old newspaper, and plain newsprint

A Country of Islands

Indonesia is the world's largest *archipelago* (group of islands). There are 13,677 to be exact! But only about 6,000 of them have people living on them, and more than half of Indonesia's entire population lives on Java.

WHAT YOU DO

•**1**• Put the wax in the tin can and melt it on the warming tray. Or, if you are using a stove, fill a pot with about an inch (2.5 cm) of water and place the can of wax in the water. With your adult helper, boil the water until the wax is melted.

•**2**• Dip the paintbrush in the hot melted wax and quickly paint the wax onto the cloth so the wax is absorbed into it. When the wax on the brush cools too much, dip it again.

   The cloth will keep its original color in the places where you paint with wax because the wax will resist the dye. To make sure that the wax has penetrated the cloth, look at the back side. If it didn't soak through, paint the same pattern on the back with more hot wax. Don't worry if this happens; it's just part of the process (A FAMILY AFFAIR, page 83)!

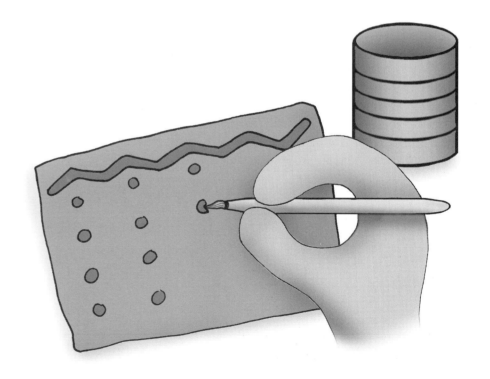

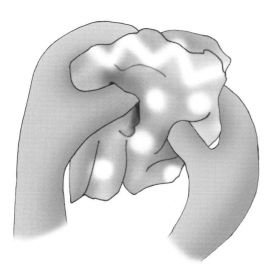

•3• Squeeze the cloth to crackle the wax and create interesting patterns of cracks. (Any wax that falls off is just extra; most of the wax is absorbed into the cloth.)

•4• With an adult helper, carefully follow the directions on the dye package to dye the cloth.

•5• To remove the wax, place the cloth between layers of plain newsprint and put several layers of regular newspaper under it (to absorb the melting wax). Iron the cloth. You can then boil the fabric if you want to get the rest of the wax out.

A Family Affair

In Java, it is traditional for women to make this batik cloth. Decorating with a canting is time-consuming, meticulous work that takes lots of practice. Young girls learn the process from their mothers by practicing waxing the back sides of their mothers' work, called "drawing through." So if your wax doesn't soak all the way through and you have to paint wax on the back, you're learning to batik just as a Javanese child would!

Do the men help with batiking, you might wonder? Well, they are in charge of dyeing the cloth. The traditional colors are made from plants: Brown comes from the bark of the soga tree and deep blue comes from indigo leaves, for example. The dyeing is done in huge vats. It is a complicated process to produce these natural colors; recipes are handed down from father to son, and sometimes the dyes don't work. The Javanese believe that if a man has an argument with his wife, the dye might fail! ✎

I bought this gorgeous sample of Javanese batik near Borobudur.

Bali Kids Make Music!

I was on Bali, an island off the eastern tip of Java, in January 1971. One day I was bicycling when I heard the sounds of a *gamelan,* an Indonesian orchestra made up of gongs, xylophones, and drums. The playing in the open-walled building in the central square was lovely. I was quite surprised to see that all the players were young children, just having fun!

Every little community in Bali has a village square, often with kids in it! The gamelans are typically set up in the open sheltered structure in the center of the square.

These Javanese kids had a friendly greeting for me as I passed their house in the pony cart on my way to Borobudur.

Around the World with Roberta

When I was in Java, I hired a pony cart to take me out to the ruins of Borobudur, a famous Buddhist monument from the ninth century. My cart had a skiddish horse — at one point it reared and started galloping up the road, the old buggy was swaying and creaking, and I was holding on for dear life! But it was exciting all the same. When the buggy was going at its normal plodding pace, there was plenty of time to say hello to the many curious and friendly children, and to watch the farmers in their rice fields. Java is near the equator, so it has a good climate for rice. I saw rice in all stages of growth: some was being planted, some was half grown, and some was being harvested.

AUSTRALIA & THE PACIFIC ISLANDS

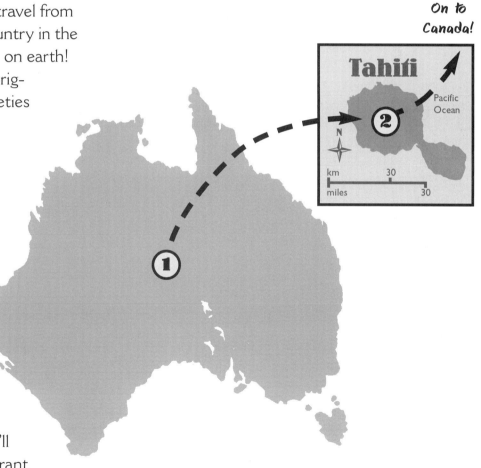

This travel adventure will be one of striking contrasts, as you travel from Australia, which has more desert for its size than any other country in the world, east across the Pacific Ocean, the largest body of water on earth!

While you might think of Australia (1) as home to "the aborigines," there were originally hundreds of distinct Aboriginal societies there, each with their own languages, ceremonies, and traditions. The continent was at one time crisscrossed with their trading routes, so that a didgeridoo (page 86) from the northern coast might turn up 1,000 miles (1,600 km) away! You'll make and play one of these traditional instruments during your stay.

Then it's off into the Pacific, heading east for a very long sail to Tahiti (2). As you travel across this vast ocean, imagine setting out in a small boat for unknown lands! Although people settled on Java (page 79) 4,000 years ago, they didn't arrive on Tahiti 6,000 miles (9,650 km) to the east for another 2,000 years! But incredibly, people made their way to every habitable island in this watery region, eventually discovering all the many thousands of them! When you land on Tahiti, you'll make a traditional feather breastplate to commemorate the vibrant island cultures of the Pacific islands.

On to Canada!

Tahiti

Pacific Ocean

N

km 30
miles 30

✴ Aboriginal Didgeridoo of Australia

This instrument has an amazing sound! The Aboriginal people of Australia have been making it for more than 40,000 years, using branches of a eucalyptus tree that has been naturally hollowed out by termites. Termites eat the wood from the inside out, so the people just have to chop off the branch, clean out the termite dung, take off the bark, and smooth the edges. To make the didgeridoo easier to play, they put beeswax around the opening to make it smoother and slightly narrower.

WHAT YOU NEED

✳ Cardboard tube, about 1" (2.5 cm) in diameter, and 3' to 5' (1 to 1.5 m) long*

✳ Colored pencils or permanent markers to decorate

*Ask at a sari shop for the cardboard tubes that sari fabrics are wrapped on. They are just perfect for this project.

WHAT YOU DO

Decorating the tube

Decorate the tube with markers and colored pencils. The Aborigines decorate with geometric designs carved into the wood. Have fun decorating this long thin tube — it's very different from drawing on flat paper!

Playing your didgeridoo

Practice blowing on the tube. You want to get the low, growly sound of a real didgeridoo. Blow pretty hard through loose lips to get the sound. If you are getting "impolite" sounds from your instrument, or you sound like an elephant, your lips are too tight. Try practicing "burbling" your lips without the tube, then continue the same thing with the tube. When you hear a low foghorn sound, you are doing the right thing, and you'll feel the whole tube vibrate in a really neat way.

If you move the end of the tube while you blow with tight lips, you'll get a buzzing bee sound! Kids who play the trumpet can use some of the same techniques on the didgeridoo. Looser lips make a lower note on the trumpet that is called a *pedal tone*. Higher notes are made with tighter lips. If you buzz your lips and hum at the same time, it is called "growling." Find a trumpet-playing friend to show you how!

It takes a lot of air to make a sound! You'll feel the whole tube vibrate when you get it right.

•SINCE LONG AGO•

In Aboriginal culture, storytelling is essential. Stories are told with dance, voice, sand painting, rock painting, and the wonderful sound of the didgeridoo. Many of these old stories are not sacred and are performed around the campfire in the evening attended by the whole community. Some of the men sing and some dance to act out the stories and myths. The dancers' bodies are decorated and the movements often imitate animals. The dances are spectacular and lots of fun. And they are a way to remember the stories from long ago and keep the culture strong.

Hear a Real Didgeridoo!

The Aboriginal people use the didgeridoo to imitate the sounds of nature, including animal sounds (calls, wings flapping, feet thumping) and the sounds of wind, trees, water, and thunder. They play long tunes with these sounds mingled into the basic drone of the instrument. It's a unique sound!

Their playing goes on for a long time, and they need a way to be able to play without having to stop the music while they breathe in! So they invented circular breathing. It involves pushing the air that is in your puffed-out cheeks down the tube while you are quickly breathing in through your nose — and it is difficult to learn!

Learn more about the didgeridoo at <**www.aboriginalart.com.au/didgeridoo/**>, the website of Aboriginal Art & Culture Centre, sponsored by a Southern Arrernte Aboriginal Tribal group of Australia. You can hear individual didgeridoo sounds (try the online lesson!) as well as download samples of traditional aboriginal music. *Werte mwarre!* (That's "please enter" in Arrernte.)

This gorgeous didgeridoo belongs to a friend of mine. It is even harder to make a sound with a real one because it is wider so you need more breath.

Taumi, or Tahitian Breastplate

Worn in battle, this braided-grass breastplate, called a *taumi,* was strong enough to repel spears, rocks, and clubs. A taumi was also very impressive-looking, and indicated the high status of the wearer. When the English explorer and navigator Captain James Cook explored the Pacific Ocean in the 1700s, he was presented with many breastplates by the generous Tahitians. The 50 breastplates Cook brought back can be seen in museums all over the world! Today these beautiful and bold breastplates are worn by Tahitian dancers and musicians when they perform traditional songs and dances.

WHAT YOU NEED

✳ Piece of tan, brown, or black felt about 11" x 15" (27 x 37 cm)

✳ Scissors

✳ Yarn needle

✳ Yarn, two 2' (60 cm) pieces

✳ 6 white pearly buttons, 1" (2.5 cm) in diameter

✳ Craft feathers (iridescent bluish or greenish black, yellow, red, black, brown) from a craft store

✳ About 120 tiny shells or white beads (or real sharks' teeth, if you can find any!)

✳ Glue stick

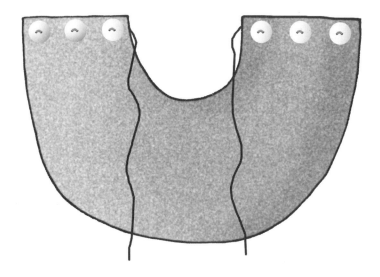

WHAT YOU DO

•**1**• Cut the piece of felt in the shape shown.

•**2**• Double-thread the needle (page 116) with yarn and knot it. Sew the three buttons (page 117) across the top on each side, starting at the outer edge. When you sew the innermost button, make sure you have at least 12" (30 cm) of yarn left over for tying on the breastplate.

•**3**• Plan your pattern of feathers and "sharks' teeth." It's traditional to make three rows of teeth and three rows of feathers. Sometimes the feathers are put on in alternating colors of red and yellow to make a spectacular design.

•**4**• Glue everything in place and let the breastplate dry. To wear your taumi, tie it at the back of your neck.

Taumi Design

A taumi was traditionally made with disks of pearly shells and three rows of feathers separated by sharks' teeth on a thick backing of braided grass and wicker slats. It took teeth from seven to 15 sharks to make one taumi. The bottom row is festooned with long white dog hair — an item of great value to the Tahitians. The native people traded bark cloth and food items for it with people who lived on islands 220 miles (352 km) away. They could only travel there in canoes during three months in the year when the winds were blowing from the correct direction.

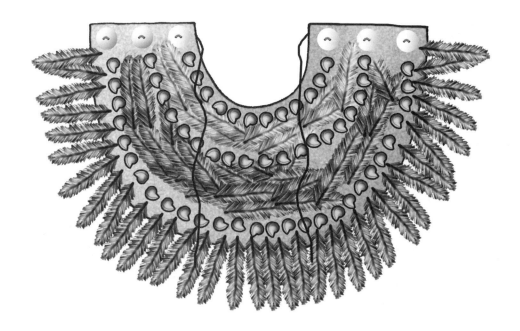

CANADA & THE UNITED STATES

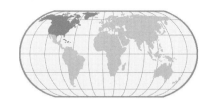

For your final travel adventure, you'll explore parts of North America. If you live in the United States or Canada, you probably think you already know what those countries are like. But you might be surprised at all the diverse cultures you'll find, from the traditions and crafts of the native peoples who have lived on the North American continent for more than 10,000 years to those of the immigrants who have come from all over the world to settle here. And you'll experience all sorts of climates — from the ice and snow of northern Canada and Alaska to the desert of the American Southwest.

You'll start your trip in Alaska (1), where you'll learn traditional native Alaskan beading styles. Then you'll travel across Canada, stopping in Nunavut (2) to make Inuit mittens and again in Ontario (3) to re-create an Algonquin birchbark canoe. When you reach the eastern United States, you'll learn the pierced-tin craft that the Pennsylvania Deutsch immigrants (4) brought from Germany, and you'll find out how one of the U.S. presidents helped start the teddy bear fad (5)! Hike through the Appalachian Mountains to a Kentucky "holler" (6) to have fun playing with an old-time wooden toy. Then it's time to head west, where you'll climb a tall mesa to a Zuni pueblo (7) and make a fetish necklace.

✳ Tlingit & Athabascan Beadwork from Alaska

The Tlingit and Athabascan Native American peoples of Alaska and western Canada are well known for their intricate beading designs. Although many eastern Native Americans started using beads in the late 1600s, they weren't available in Alaska until the first Russian and Hudson Bay Company traders brought them to the area in the mid-1700s. It was another 100 years before the smaller colorful glass beads became common. Since then the native people have used these beads to adorn moccasins, clothing, bags, and dance regalia.

Beading work was originally done by women, but today both men and women do beadwork in traditional patterns. The modern-day Tlingit typically make designs of eagles, frogs, and other animals; the Athabascans usually make beautiful patterns of flowers and leaves.

Try your hand at beading your favorite animal or flower, or create an abstract design!

WHAT YOU NEED

* Paper and colored pencils or chalk
* Felt cloth, any color, about 3" x 4" (7.5 x 10 cm)
* Thread
* Beading needle (very long and thin to go through tiny beads; available at craft stores)
* Seed beads (tiny beads available from craft stores)
* Scissors

WHAT YOU DO

•**1**• Sketch your design on the paper. Traditional designs were often plants or animals, but you can draw anything you like! Lightly copy the design to the felt, if you want, with the colored pencils or chalk.

•**2**• Double-thread the needle (page 116). Push the needle through from the back of the felt so it comes up in the design. Pull the thread tight.

•**3**• Thread one, two, or three beads in a color that corresponds to your design onto the needle. Slide them onto the thread. Lay the beaded thread down so the beads follow your design and push the needle back down through the cloth, pulling the thread tight.

•**4**• Push the needle back up through the cloth to the front side so it comes up next to where the thread just went down. Stitch several more beads in place. Continue working section by section, adding a few beads at a time, to complete your design. If you run out of thread, knot the thread ends on the back side of the fabric. Rethread the needle and continue beading.

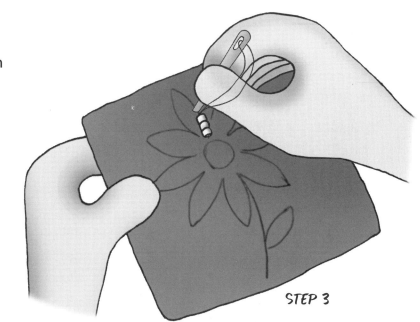

STEP 3

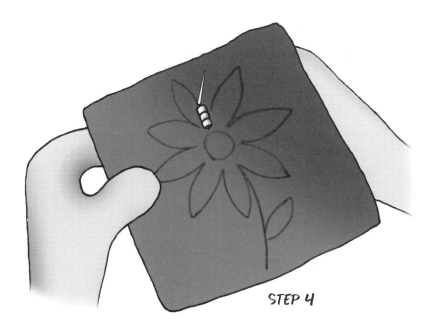

STEP 4

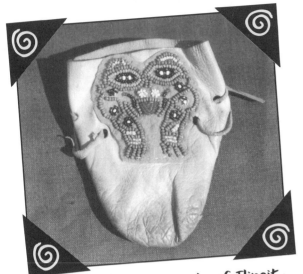

I bought this example of Tlingit beading in the tiny village of Hoonah, Alaska. It was made to decorate the top of a Tlingit-style moccasin.

In the 1970s, I lived in Juneau, Alaska, and taught a cultural education program sponsored by the Alaska State Museum. I learned a lot about the traditional crafts and lifestyle from the older people in nearby villages, who were very gracious and welcomed me into their homes. Then I taught my new skills to groups of White and Tlingit kids from Juneau.

I especially enjoyed the Jameses, a Tlinglit family who lived right next to the Alaska Native Brotherhood Hall where I held classes. One day one of the James girls shyly asked if I could loan some money to her mom. I was glad to give them the modest amount of money that they requested, but I didn't want them to feel embarrassed about owing me money. Luckily, I remembered that Mrs. James did beautiful beadwork. I gave her extra money to buy beads, and she made me this beaded eagle. We were both happy!

Crafty Idea!

The Native Americans used sinew as thread. *Sinew* is made from the tendon of a animal, such as a deer. It has to be moistened so it is flexible enough to sew with, but it can be split into fine thread that is almost as thin as cotton thread and is very strong. If you can't find it at a local craft store, here is a source: <**www.wakeda.com/simsingensin.html**>.

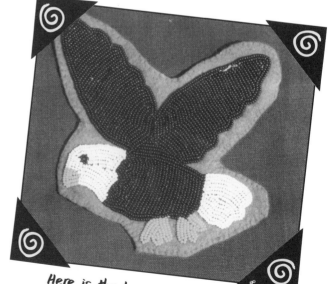

Here is the beautiful eagle that Mrs. James made for me.

Inuit Mittens from Nunavut

For thousands of years, the Inuit (EE-new-eet, meaning "the People"), the native people of northern Canada and Alaska, have withstood amazingly cold weather by wearing clothing that was perfectly designed for their environment. Traditionally, their hooded parkas and trousers were made of two layers of caribou or sealskin. The inner layer had the furry side facing in to trap air for warmth and to wick away moisture from sweat before it made the person feel cold. The outer layer was worn fur side out, making it easy to brush the snow off. They wore *mukluks* (knee-high boots), and of course they wore mittens.

In the old days, the Inuit made their boots and mittens out of caribou or sealskin as well, tanning the skins to make them waterproof. Now they make mittens with all kinds of fur, such as seal, beaver, raccoon, and rabbit. Sometimes the kids' mittens are connected together with a long string that goes through the arms of their parkas. Try unwrapping a gift wearing your big mittens, a holiday game Inuit children sometimes play!

WHAT YOU NEED

* Pattern-making supplies: tracing paper, pencil, craft scissors, manila folder or heavy paper

* Straight pins

* Fake fur, fleece, or real fur, such as sheepskin from a worn-out car seat cover, 2 pieces about 9" x 12" (22.5 x 30 cm) each

* Pen

* Fabric scissors

* Needle and thread

The Inuit Homeland

Nunavut (meaning "Our Land" in Inuktitut, the language of the Inuit) became a separate self-governing territory of Canada on April 1, 1999. This huge area has been the Inuit homeland for thousands of years; with this move, Inuit rights to this land were officially returned. The Inuit now govern themselves, and can actively preserve their culture, keeping their traditional values while at the same time embracing the best of the modern world.

WHAT YOU DO

•**1**• Trace the MITTEN THUMB, MITTEN PALM, and MITTEN BACK patterns (pages 120 to 122) and cut them out carefully. Now trace each tracing-paper pattern onto the manila folder or heavy paper and cut it out. Label each pattern as shown.

•**2**• Pin the patterns, labeled side *up,* to one piece of cloth. Pay attention to the direction of the nap (GO WITH THE FLOW!, page 97). If you place the pattern pieces close together as shown, you can get a whole mitten out of each piece of cloth.

•**3**• With the pen, trace around each pattern carefully. Remove the patterns and cut out the mitten pieces.

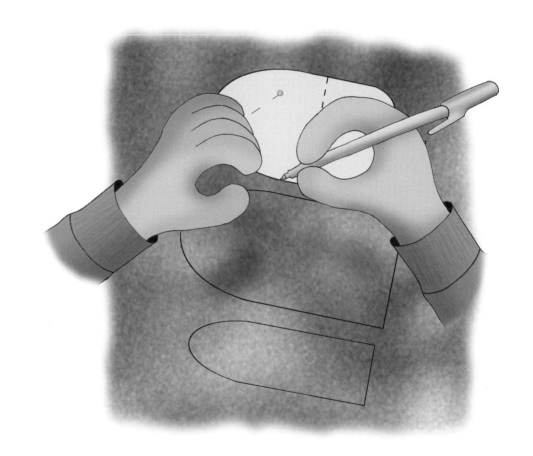

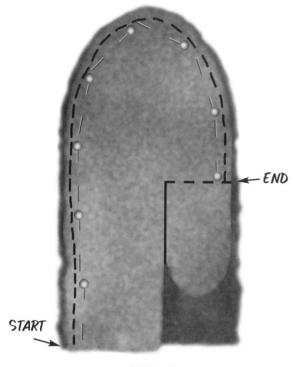

← END

START →

STEP 5

STEP 6

•4• Pin the patterns to the other piece of cloth, labeled side *down*. Trace and cut out the pieces for your second mitten.

•5• For each mitten, pin the right sides (the sides that will face out) of the mitten back and the mitten palm together. Double-thread the needle (page 116) and use a running stitch (page 117) to sew them together. Start sewing at the wrist and up the side of the mitten to where the thumb flap bends (shown as a dotted line on the pattern). Snip the thread and double-knot it (page 116).

•6• Fold up each thumb flap on the mitten palms and pin the mitten thumbs to the thumb flaps. You may need a little adult help here; the thumbs are slightly different sizes so you'll need to bunch up the larger thumb piece slightly as you pin to make the edges meet.

⠿ **Go with the Flow!** ⠿

Most kinds of real fur have nap, which means that one direction is smoother and one is rougher, as if the fur "flows" in one direction. You'll notice this when you pet a cat, and the cat will notice if you pet it the wrong way! If you are using fur with nap, place the pattern on the fur so that the arrow for "direction of nap" points in the smooth direction.

•**7**• Start at the wrist and sew around the thumb piece and down to the wrist. Don't worry if your seams are a little uneven — your mittens will still be wearable! Snip the thread and double-knot it. Turn each mitten right side out and try it on.

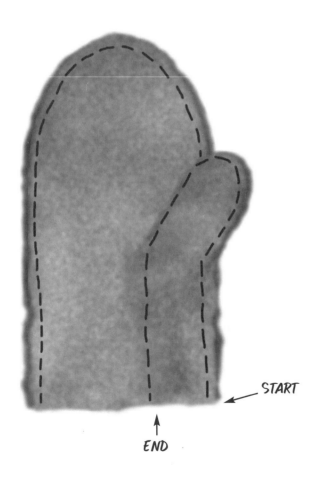

START

END

Inuit Clothing of Today

In some isolated places, Inuit clothing has remained very traditional, but for the most part, styles have changed since the late 1800s. The clothing of the Yupik (YUP-ik), the Inuit of western Alaska, for example, has adopted a number of Western features. Parkas have changed from a pullover design to one with a front zippered closing, and women's parkas now have a short ruffled skirt attached to the bottom. A brightly colored cloth version of the old pullover parka, the *kuspuk* has become the accepted dress for traditional dancing. The cloth parka is the most common piece of traditional Alaskan dress, worn not only by many Yupik, but by other Alaskan natives and by Whites. With its unique amalgamation of Native and Western design, it's a practical method for staying warm as well as an expression of local pride.

Algonquin Birch-Bark Canoe

The birch-bark canoe was an essential tool for the first inhabitants of the area we now call Canada. The land was thick with brush and trees, and the easiest way to get around was on the many rivers and lakes. Strong but lightweight, birch-bark canoes were well suited to going down the rapidly flowing rivers. And when a particular lake ended or a river became too narrow to travel, the birch-bark canoe was light enough to be easily *portaged* (carried) to the next body of water. The European explorers and fur traders who came to eastern Canada soon learned from the native peoples like the Algonquin Indians about the wonderful properties of the birch-bark canoe, and it quickly became essential to them, too.

Here's how to make a miniature canoe that will actually float!

WHAT YOU NEED

* Pattern-making supplies: tracing paper, pencil, craft scissors, manila folder or heavy paper
* Stiff white vinyl cloth or piece of old window shade, 4" x 6" (10 x 15 cm)
* Fabric scissors
* Crewel or embroidery needle (with a sharp point and large eye) from a craft or fabric store
* 2 pieces of thick thread, 3' (1 m) long
* 12" (30 cm) pipe cleaner
* Stick of chewing gum or modeling clay
* Small pebbles

WHAT YOU DO

•**1**• Trace the CANOE pattern (page 123) onto tracing paper and cut it out. Trace the tracing-paper pattern onto the manila folder or heavy paper and cut it out. Label the pattern. (And start chewing your gum!)

•**2**• Trace the pattern onto the vinyl. Cut it out.

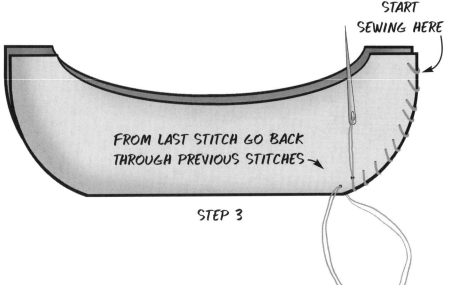

START SEWING HERE

FROM LAST STITCH GO BACK THROUGH PREVIOUS STITCHES →

STEP 3

•**3**• Double-thread the needle (page 116). Fold together one end of the canoe, matching the edges evenly. Using the whipstitch (page 118), sew down to the fold. Then, from the back side, bring the needle through the previous hole.

•**4**• Continue sewing back up through the same holes, forming a series of V's.

The Traditional Algonquin Canoe

The Algonquin were one of the native groups who relied heavily on the birch-bark canoe. When the French came to Canada in the 1600s, the Algonquin shared skills and traded with them. The French fur traders were known as *voyageurs* (the French word for "travelers") because they traveled all over the north country of Canada, using two handy methods of year-round transportation they learned about from the Algonquin: the toboggan and — you guessed it! — the birch-bark canoe!

The traditional Algonquin birch-bark canoe is made by sewing the sheets of birch bark onto a cedar frame using very thin pieces of spruce root. The cracks are sealed with pitch pine and grease. The gunwales are made from cedar logs.

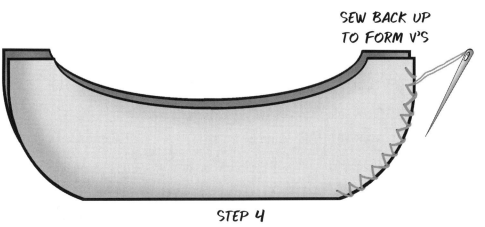

SEW BACK UP TO FORM V'S

STEP 4

5 Sew three more whipstitches as shown. Don't cut the thread.

6 Fold the pipe cleaner in half and tuck the folded end into the three stitches you just made. Continue stitching to sew one half of the pipe cleaner to the *gunwale* (the upper edge of the side of the canoe, pronounced "gunnel"). When you get to the other end, tie a strong knot.

7 Repeat steps 3, 4, and 5 to finish the other end and side. Tuck the two ends of the pipe cleaner under the three stitches in step 5 to hold them in place. Shape the gunwales so the boat is about 2" (5 cm) wide.

8 Take your well-chewed gum or clay and form it into two lumps, each 1" (2.5 cm) long. Push the lumps firmly into the *bow* (front) and *stern* (rear) seams, down at the bottom, to keep water from leaking into your boat. Test it out in the water. You may have to add more gum or pebbles for *ballast* (weight) so it doesn't tip. (Isn't it interesting that you have to *add* weight to the canoe to keep it from sinking!)

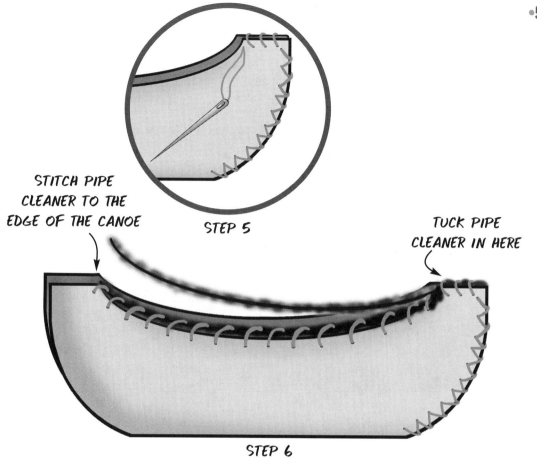

STEP 5

STITCH PIPE CLEANER TO THE EDGE OF THE CANOE

TUCK PIPE CLEANER IN HERE

STEP 6

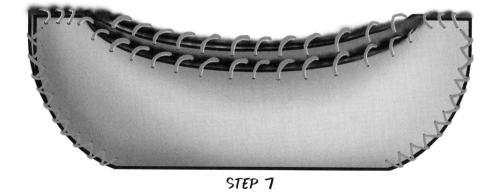

STEP 7

Add a Paddler!

You can easily shape a little figure for your canoe out of a 22" (30 cm) piece of flexible wire. Fold the piece of wire in half and form a circle for a head at the fold. Bend and twist the wire to form the arms, body, and legs. Tape on a paper face. Give your wire person a Popsicle-stick paddle and he's on his way! You may have to adjust how wide the canoe is or add more ballast to keep it afloat.

The Algonquin Today

There are currently almost 8,000 Algonquin living today in Quebec and Ontario, where they are actively working to preserve their language, culture, and territory. To learn more about their history as well as their lifestyle of today, take on online tour of the Algonquin Nation by visiting <**www.algonquinnation.ca**> and clicking on "Take the Tour."

Pennsylvania Deutsch–Style Pierced Tin

You've probably heard of keeping money in a safe, but how about pies? Long ago, like other farming people, the Pennsylvania Deutsch would sometimes eat pie for breakfast, lunch, and dinner. (Doesn't that sound wonderful!) Several times a week the women in the family would make dozens of different kinds of pies. They didn't have refrigerators, so they kept the pies in special cupboards called *pie safes*. These had tin sides that were perforated with tiny holes to allow air circulation, while keeping the pies safe from pesky mice and insects. The holes were made in beautiful patterns with a hammer and nails. Some traditional patterns were tulips, hearts, sunflowers, chickens, diamonds, circles, and stars.

You can use the same technique to create an intricate design on tin that you can frame and hang on the wall.

WHAT YOU NEED

* ✳ Scissors
* ✳ Disposable aluminum pie pans or roasting pans
* ✳ Pencil and scrap paper
* ✳ Frame (FOR THE FRAME, page 104)
* ✳ Masking tape
* ✳ Cardboard (to protect your work surface)
* ✳ Small nail and hammer

WHAT YOU DO

•**1**• Cut the aluminum to the right size to fit the opening in the center of your frame. Tape the sharp edges.

•**2**• To plan your pattern, sketch the design on the scrap paper.

•**3**• Place the aluminum on the cardboard protector and use the hammer and nail to poke your pattern in the metal. (You can lay your sketch on top of the aluminum if you want to copy it exactly.) Hammer just enough so the tip of the nail pierces the aluminum. You don't want the nail to go through the cardboard (and into the table). If your aluminum is thin, you may be able to push the nail in by hand.

•**4**• When the pattern is complete, turn it over and gently hammer down any sharp places created by the nail.

•**5**• Tape the aluminum in place behind the frame. You can now decorate the frame if you like.

::::: For the Frame :::::

Recycled plastic foam is a good material for your frame. Black plastic-foam trays (the kind produce is sold on) look especially nice. You can also cut a piece of cardboard to the overall size you want and then cut out an opening in the center.

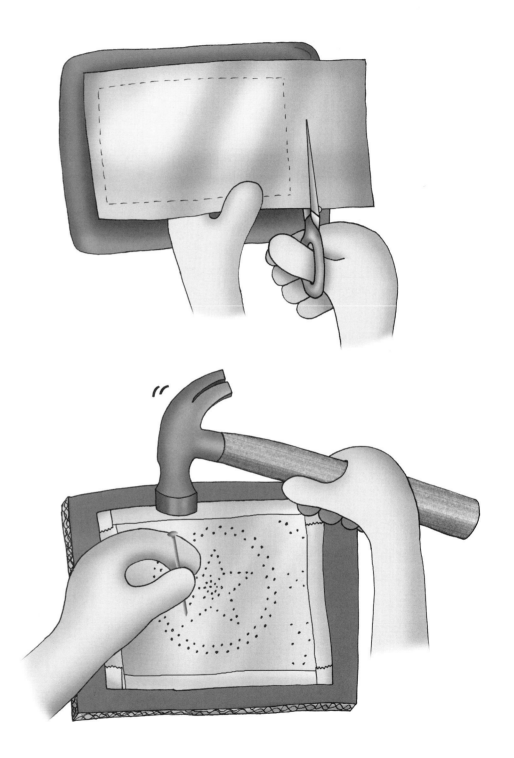

The Pennsylvania Dutch ... Make that Deutsch!

Dutch people are from Holland, but the Pennsylvania "Dutch" actually came from Germany and the German-speaking part of Switzerland in the early 1700s to settle in Pennsylvania. The confusion came about because the word *Deutsch* (the German word for "German") sounded like the word Dutch to the non–German-speaking Americans.

The Pennsylvania Deutsch women are great pie-bakers to this day! One traditional type is called shoofly pie, made with lots of molasses and brown sugar.

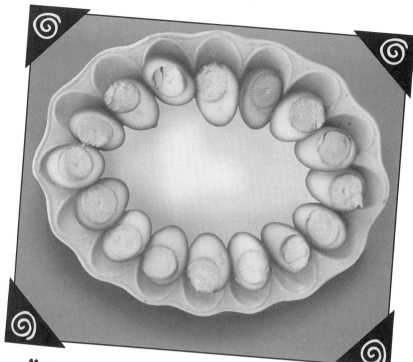

My mom would make these traditional Pennsylvania Deutsch purple eggs for us when we were growing up.

Around the World with Roberta

My mother is Pennsylvania Deutsch, but I never knew very much about her childhood. Both her parents died when she was young and she was raised by her aunt. Recently, I took a trip with my mother back to Pennsylvania and met her oldest childhood friend. After 60 years, they still liked each other! My mother's friend served us purple eggs, a traditional Pennsylvania Deutsch dish. To make them, you peel hardboiled eggs and soak them overnight in the juice from a jar of pickled beets. When you cut them in half the next day, you see the bright yellow center and the purple dyed outside, with pure white in between. They're quite colorful — and they taste good, too!

✳ All-American Teddy Bear

Teddy bears are named after Theodore Roosevelt, president of the United States from 1901 to 1909, whose nickname was Teddy. President Roosevelt was a hunter. In 1902 he went on a bear hunt but refused to shoot the only bear the hunting party saw. A cartoonist made a cartoon showing a little scared bear, and that inspired the name "Teddy's bear" for stuffed bears. The bear toys became very popular — and Teddy bears are still a favorite toy today! These small teddy bears are surprisingly easy to make — and very lovable!

WHAT YOU NEED

* *Pattern-making supplies:* tracing paper, pencil, craft scissors, manila folder or heavy paper
* Felt-tip marker or chalk
* Furry cloth (fleece scraps or sections of an old sweatshirt turned inside out are perfect), 2 pieces at least 7" x 8" (17.5 x 20 cm) each or large piece at least 14" x 16" (35 x 40 cm)
* Fabric scissors
* Straight pins
* Needle and thread
* Stuffing
* Shiny beads, wiggly eyes, buttons, or permanent markers
* Cloth scraps of felt or old jeans, shirt cuffs, tops from old socks, cloth ribbon

WHAT YOU DO

To make the bear

•1• Trace the TEDDY BEAR pattern (page 119) and cut it out. Now trace the tracing-paper pattern onto the manila folder or heavy paper and cut it out. Label the pattern.

•2• With the marker or chalk, carefully trace the paper pattern onto the cloth twice to make a front and back.

•3• Cut out the two pieces. You may want grown-up help with this step, because it is a lot easier to sew the bear if the two halves are exactly the same. (The finished bear will look nicer, too!)

An "Earthquake" of a President!

Teddy Roosevelt was a well-loved president; he believed in working hard for worthy causes and accomplished a lot. A devoted conservationist, he created 150 National Forests and five National Parks and put a total of 230 million acres (92,000,000 h) under federal protection. He also won the Nobel Peace Prize in 1905 for his diplomatic efforts after the Russo-Japanese War. Roosevelt had so much energy that his friend Buffalo Bill Cody called him "a cyclone," and his friend Mark Twain called him "an earthquake."

•**4**• Place the right sides (the side that would normally face out) of the cloth together. With fleece, you won't have to worry about this step, because both sides are the same. If you are using an old sweatshirt, use the inside for the outside of the bear so the bear will be soft and fuzzy. Pin the pieces together.

•**5**• Double-thread the needle (page 116). Using a running stitch (page 117), sew around the edge from the tip of one toe around the whole body to the tip of the other toe. Leave the crotch open.

•**6**• Snip the threads so you can remove the needle and tie a double knot (page 116) at the ends.

STEP 4

STEP 5

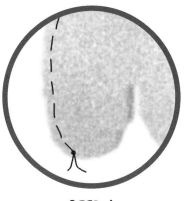

STEP 6

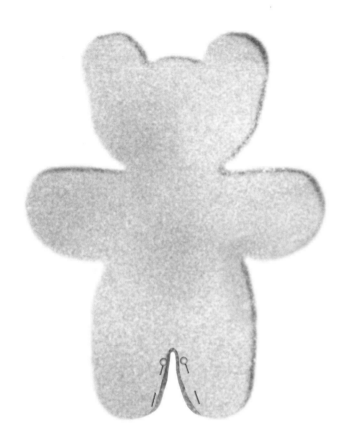

To make the face

You can draw on the face with fine-tip permanent markers or fabric paint if your cloth is thin or smooth. Or you can sew or glue on bead eyes or wiggly eyes, and sew on a flat two-hole button (page 117) for a snout. Button holes look like nostrils!

To make clothes

A sock top makes a nice tube skirt.

To make a long or short vest, use the TEDDY BEAR VEST pattern (page 120).

Use the TEDDY BEAR HAT pattern (page 120) and a small circle of stiff material to make a hat.

•**7**• Turn the bear right side out. Stuff little bits of stuffing into the ears, head, and arms. Use a pencil to poke the stuffing in, if necessary. Then fill the fat belly and the legs.

•**8**• Fold the unsewn edges in as shown and pin them in place.

•**9**• Thread your needle again and whipstitch (page 118) from toe to toe. Tie a firm knot.

·You Are Here·

✳ Appalachian Flip-Flop Toy

Back in the 1700s and 1800s, colonial American children were expected to spend their Sundays very quietly. They could only play with "Sunday toys" (toys with a Christian element). One example was a toy Noah's ark with all the pairs of animals. Another such toy was a Jacob's ladder, a perpetual-motion toy that we now also call the flip-flop toy. There is something so amazing about this old-fashioned toy that even after you have made one, you may still catch yourself thinking, "How *do* they make it?" — until you suddenly remember that you made it yourself!

To play with your flip-flop toy, hold one end up and flip the top block over. The rest of the blocks will flip-flop down until they can go no farther. Then tilt the top block over the other way and they will flip-flop down again.

WHAT YOU NEED

✳ Sandpaper

✳ 6 to 8 wooden blocks, each about 2" x 3" (5 x 7.5 cm) and ¹/₄" (5 mm) thick from scrap wood*

✳ Scissors

✳ Ruler

✳ Cloth ribbon less than ¹/₂" (1 cm) wide, 9' to 12' (2.7 to 3.6 m) long

✳ Glue gun or craft or carpenter's glue

✳ Crayons, colored pens or markers (optional)

Kamaboko boards (pine boards that hold a Japanese-style fish cake) are perfect for this project. Ask at an Asian grocery store. Eat the kamaboko, wash the board, and (with an adult's help) saw it evenly in half.

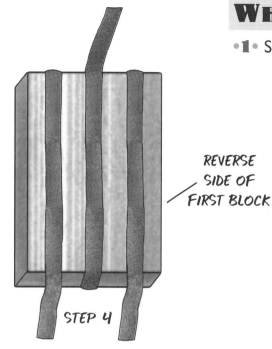

1¼"
(3 CM)

TOP SIDE

1"
(2.5 CM)

STEP 3

REVERSE
SIDE OF
FIRST BLOCK

STEP 4

What You Do

•1• Sand the edges of the wood until they are smooth.

•2• Cut the ribbon to 6" (15 cm) lengths.

•3• Glue three pieces of ribbon to each block as shown, applying wide strips of glue to the wood and pressing the ribbons down firmly. Leave the last block plain. If you are using craft glue, let it dry for 10 minutes.

•4• Fold the ribbons of the first block around the wood as shown.

•5• Hold the next block with the ribbons out and the blank side up as shown.
Place it on top of the first block, lining up the ribbons as shown. Glue the short ends from the first block onto the top (blank) side of second block. Pull the ribbons taut before pressing them firmly down into the glue.

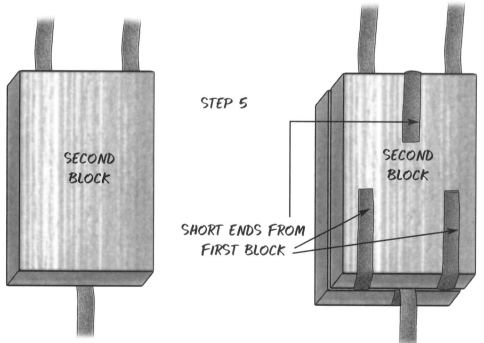

STEP 5

SECOND
BLOCK

SECOND
BLOCK

SHORT ENDS FROM
FIRST BLOCK

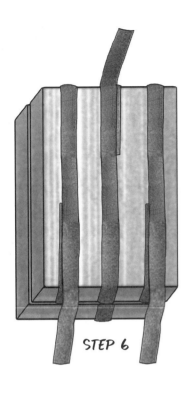

STEP 6

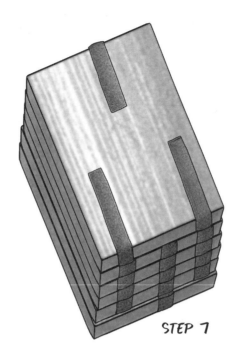

STEP 7

•6• Fold the long ribbons down over the second block (they will cover the short ends you just glued in place). Repeat step 5.

•7• Continue until you reach the last block, the one with no long ribbons attached. Place it on top and glue the short ends to it. You're finished! If you used white glue, let the blocks dry for at least 20 minutes.

•8• Decorate the wood in fun patterns using crayons, colored pencils, or markers if desired.

Around the World with Roberta

One fall while I was in college, I lived with Arminda Stacy and her kids in a Kentucky "holler" (what the country folk there call a hollow, or small valley) in Appalachia, a rural region of the southeastern United States. Her husband had been killed the year before in a coal-mine accident. I helped Arminda dig potatoes, milk the cow, call the chickens down from the hills, and iron mountains of clothes. (I became famous as the fastest ironer in the holler!) I also helped the teacher at the one-room schoolhouse, a winding walk away up the holler.

It was a very wonderful time for me. Arminda was 40 and I was 20. I was a college student and she couldn't read, but we laughed and talked and worked together hour after hour, like sisters. Her kids were lots of fun too. Alice Ruth was only 1; Evelyn, 2; Pamela Kay, 6; Ola and Zola, 8; Pollard, 9; Sithy Jane, 10; Louis and Lois, 12; Kathy Ann, 14 and Carter, 15. Her other five kids had grown up and left home.

Zuni Fetish Necklace

The Native Americans of the Southwest make and use animal *fetishes* (objects believed to have magical powers that help or protect their owners). Sometimes people find rocks that are shaped like an animal, but usually they carve the animal out of shell, stone, antler, or wood.

The Zuni of western New Mexico are known for being especially skilled at carving. Bears, mountain lions, badgers, wolves, eagles, and moles are considered spirit animals that help with hunting, cure disease, and solve other problems. And, just for the fun of carving, some Zuni carvers also make rabbits, owls, turtles, frogs, and snakes, even though those animals are not considered to have magical powers.

You can have fun creating your own animal art in the form of a beautiful (and lucky!) necklace.

Zuni Homes

The Zuni people have lived in what's now southern New Mexico for thousands of years. Their homes, called *pueblos,* are flat-roofed and several stories tall. They're made from *adobe* (mud-and-water bricks baked in the sun). To get upstairs, you climb up a ladder that leans against the outside wall and step onto the front porch that is actually the roof for the house below! All over what is now the American Southwest there are many similar pueblos built into cliffs or set atop flat-topped mountains called *mesas*. Most of those villages were abandoned during the thirteenth century during a long drought, but the Zuni continue to live in their protected pueblos and keep their age-old values and traditions.

WHAT YOU NEED

✴ Air-drying or polymer clay in several colors (CHOOSING A CLAY, right)
✴ Metal stick such as a knitting needle or kitchen skewer, or a sharp pencil
✴ Strong thread, 20" (50 cm)
✴ Beads in your favorite colors

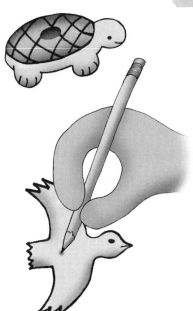

WHAT YOU DO

•1• Form small lumps of the clay into animal shapes. Don't make any really narrow parts because they will probably break off. Make at least three animal fetishes for your necklace.

•2• Push the metal stick or the pencil through the animal shape to make a hole.

•3• If you aren't using air-drying clay, ask an adult to bake the animal beads for you, following the directions on the clay package.

•4• String the beads and the animal shapes onto the thread. Knot the ends.

···· Choosing a Clay ····

Air-drying or self-hardening clays, like Crayola Model Magic, are very easy to shape, and they don't stain your clothing or work surface. These nontoxic clays harden to a firm consistency in 24 to 36 hours without baking.

Polymer clays like Sculpey or Fimo are actually made of plastic. They don't dry out when exposed to the air, so to harden your finished shapes, you'll need to bake them in the oven. Always wash your hands after working with polymer clays. Bake them (with adult help) in a well-ventilated area following the package instructions and cool them outdoors if possible; their fumes are toxic.

Unbaked polymer clay will stain and can damage the finish on a wooden table or countertop. An empty cereal box, flattened out, makes a good work surface.

I bought this colorful Zuni necklace with it's bright blue, white, deep purple, and black turtles as a birthday present for myself at a Native American fair.

I was fortunate enough to visit the Acoma Pueblo in New Mexico. It sits 400 feet (120 m) up on a mesa that has nearly vertical walls and only the space of about one or two city blocks on top! Yet in that space are lots of houses, as well as several natural rainwater basins that once supplied the community with all the water it needed. To climb down from the mesa we took the old trail, possibly the same one used since the eighth century when the pueblo was first inhabited! It is very steep and very narrow between walls of sandstone. The location protected the Acoma from invaders until 1947, when the native people agreed to let a Hollywood film crew build a road to the top and make a movie there! One really sad consequence of that decision was that the dust from the road has made the water in the basins dirty and undrinkable.

Naturally Bright!

Zuni-carved animals come in surprisingly bright colors because of very colorful natural rocks and shells of the Southwest. Turquoise is bright blue and malachite is green, for example. Serpentine is yellow and green, and amber is reddish yellow. And mother-of-pearl and abalone are a beautiful shiny iridescent white. So the bright colors of your clay are not too unnatural!

STITCHES & KNOTS

Use this illustrated guide to quickly learn simple sewing and embroidery stitches and any knots you'll need to know to complete the crafts in this book.

Backstitch

Knot the thread and bring the needle up through the fabric. Take a small backward stitch, inserting the needle behind the thread. Now bring the needle up ahead of the thread and pull the thread through. Repeat this pattern, always starting each stitch behind the previous one. To finish, stitch through the last stitch a second time; knot the thread on the back side of the fabric and snip it off close to the knot.

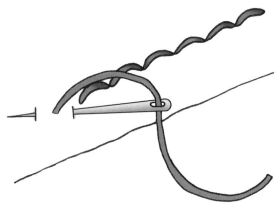

Double Knot

Use this knot to tie two ends of thread together when you finish stitching using a double-threaded needle, or for tying two ends of rope together.

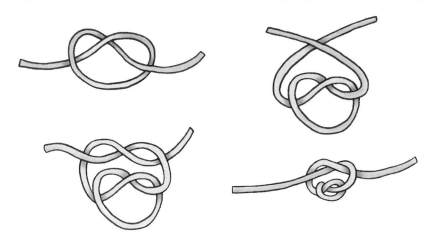

Double-Thread the Needle

To form an extra-strong double strand of thread, thread the needle and knot the two ends together.

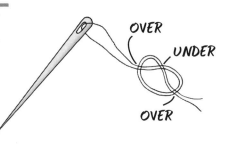

OVER
UNDER
OVER

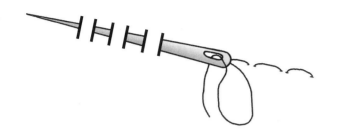

Running Stitch

Use these short, even stitches to hand-stitch a seam. Knot the thread and bring the needle up through the fabric. Work the needle in and out to make three or four stitches, then pull the thread through all the stitches. Continue until you finish the seam. Knot the thread on the wrong side of the fabric and snip the thread close to the knot.

Sew on a Button

Double-thread the needle and knot the ends. Bring the needle up from the underside of the fabric to where you want to sew on the button and pull the thread all the way through one of the buttonholes. Insert the needle through another hole in the button and down through the fabric again, pulling the thread all the way through. Repeat this up-and-down stitching through all the holes of the button until it is secure.

To finish, wrap the thread three times around the threads between the button and the fabric. Insert the needle close to the threads and pull it through to the underside of the fabric. Knot the thread and cut it.

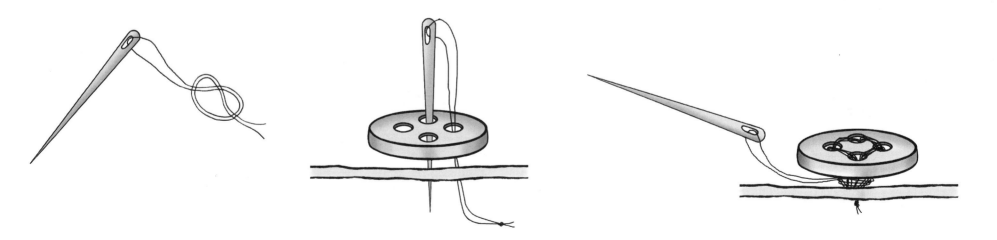

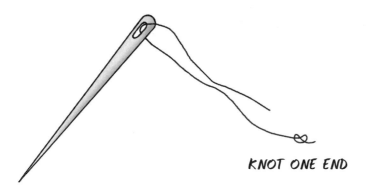

KNOT ONE END

Single-Thread the Needle

Thread the needle. Knot one of the ends.

Whipstitch

Thread the needle and knot it. Bring the needle from the wrong side of the fabric to the right side to hide the knot. Pull the needle through both pieces of fabric and pull the thread all the way through so it pulls the two edges together. Continue sewing with small, tight stitches, always bringing the needle through from the same side, until the seam is closed. To finish, slip the needle through the last couple of stitches you made a few times and pull the thread tight; cut it off close to the fabric.

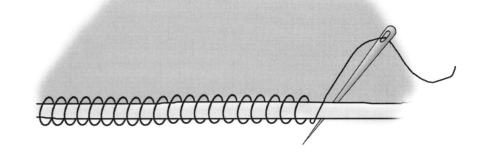

PATTERNS

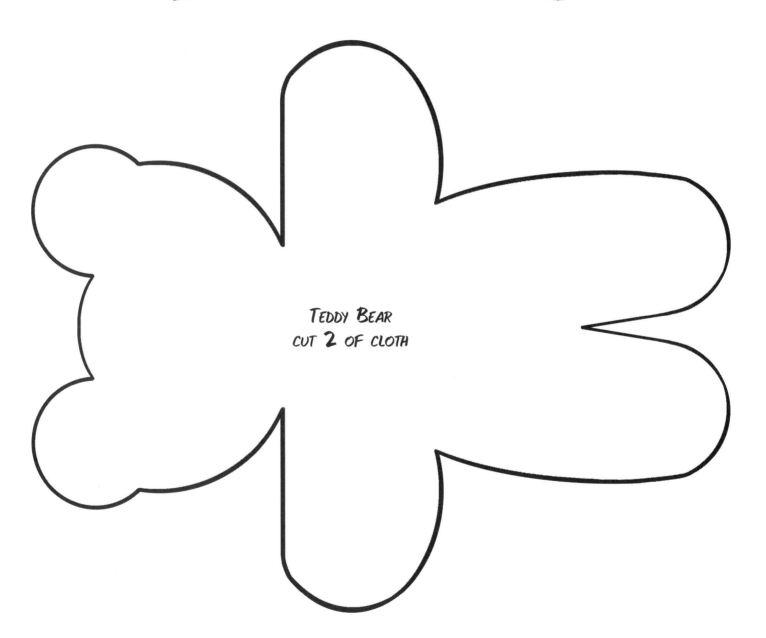

TEDDY BEAR
CUT **2** OF CLOTH

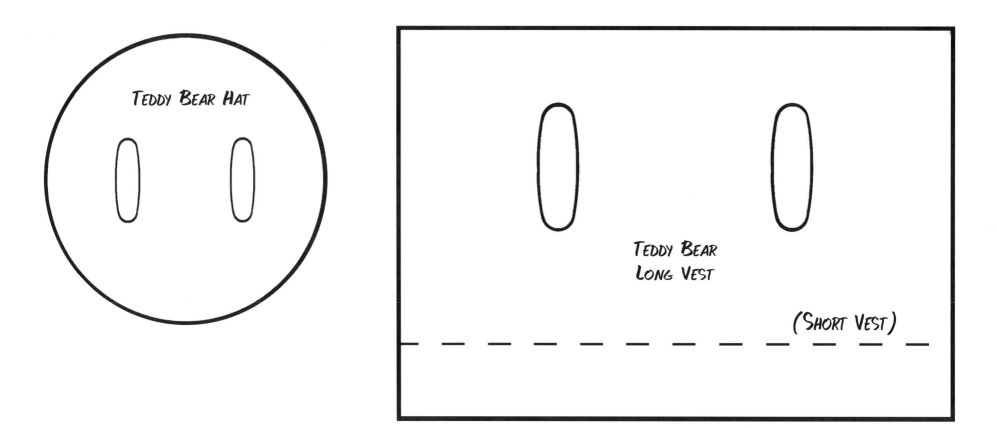

TEDDY BEAR HAT

TEDDY BEAR
LONG VEST

(SHORT VEST)

MITTEN THUMB
(CUT 2 OF CLOTH)
DIRECTION OF NAP

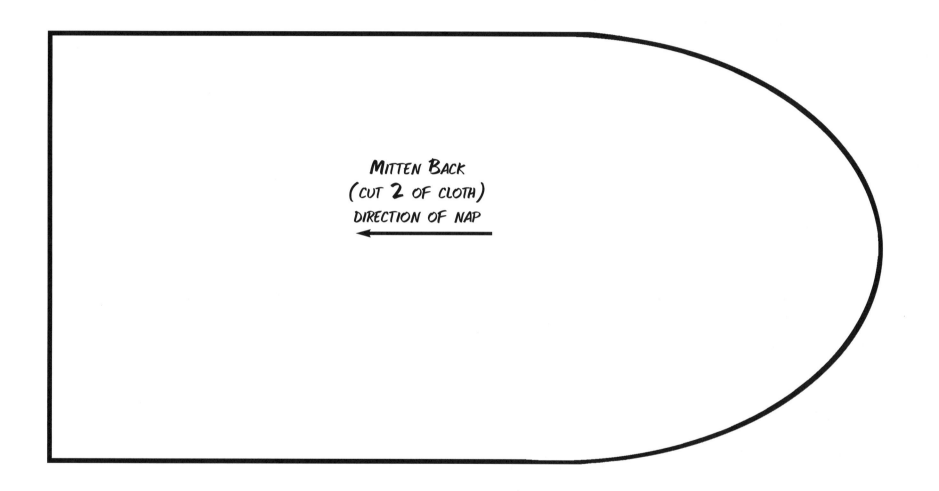

MITTEN BACK
(CUT **2** OF CLOTH)
DIRECTION OF NAP

←

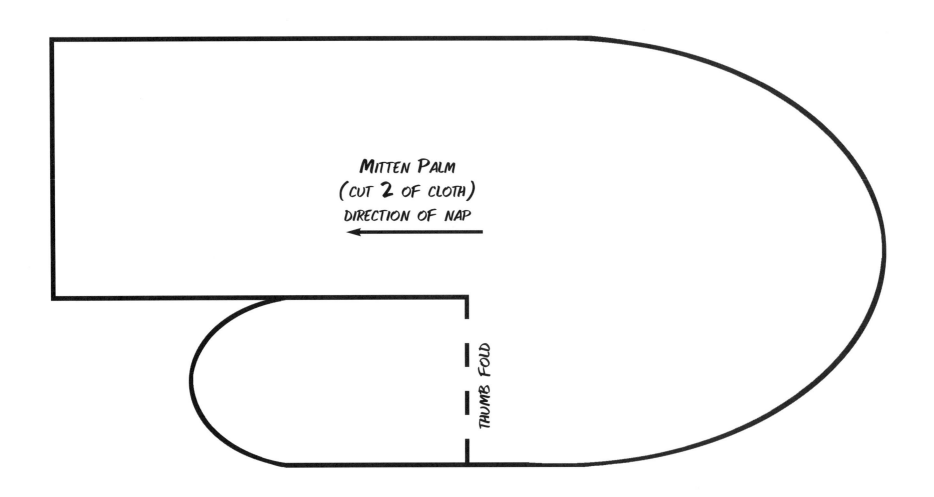

MITTEN PALM
(CUT **2** OF CLOTH)
DIRECTION OF NAP

THUMB FOLD

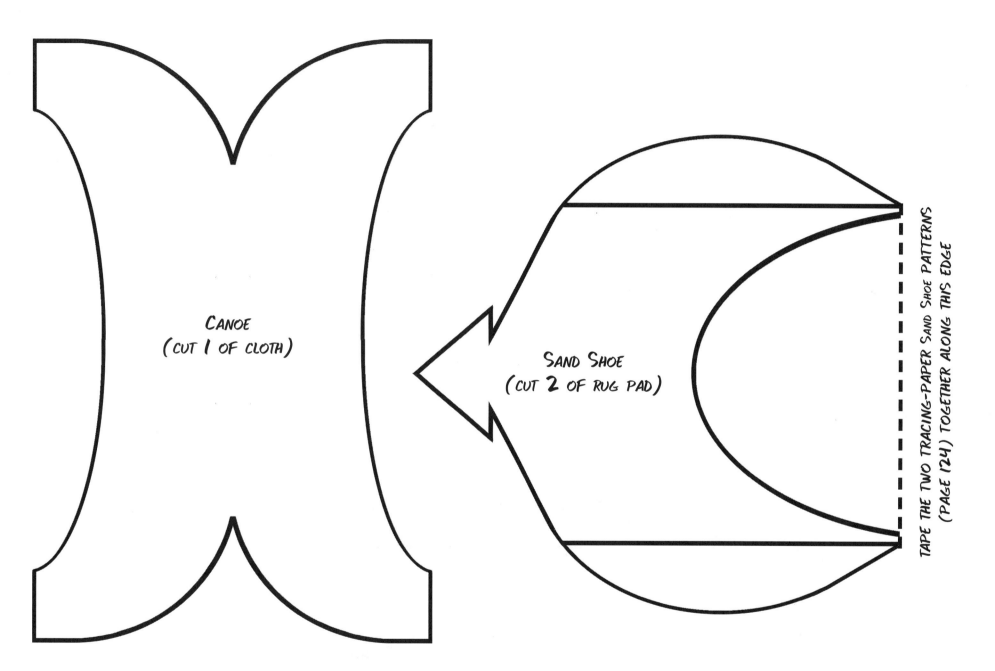

Canoe
(cut 1 of cloth)

Sand Shoe
(cut 2 of rug pad)

TAPE THE TWO TRACING-PAPER SAND SHOE PATTERNS
(PAGE 124) TOGETHER ALONG THIS EDGE

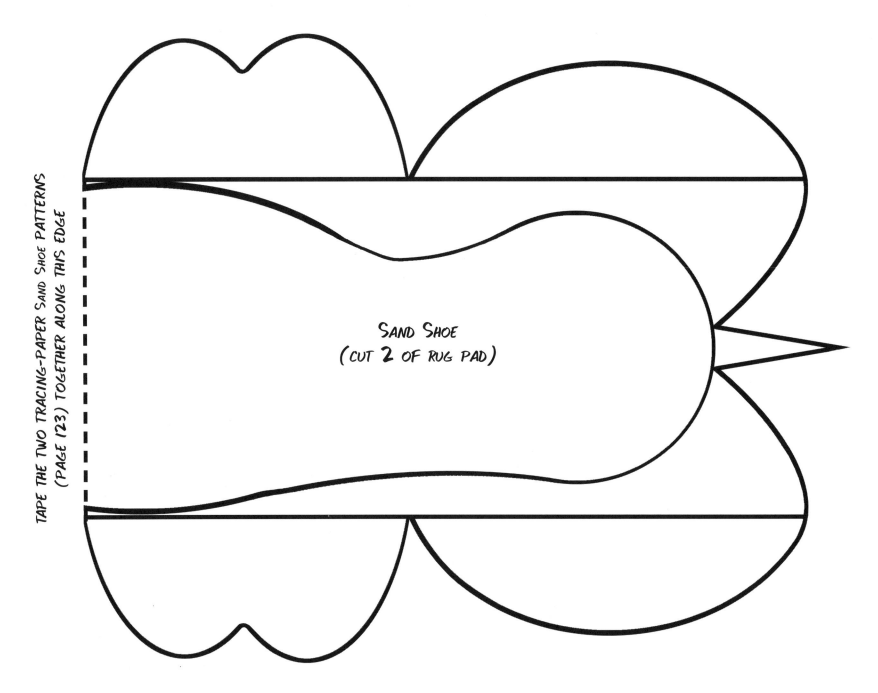

TAPE THE TWO TRACING-PAPER SAND SHOE PATTERNS (PAGE 123) TOGETHER ALONG THIS EDGE

SAND SHOE
(CUT **2** OF RUG PAD)

INDEX

More Good Books from Williamson Publishing

Williamson books are available from your bookseller or directly from Williamson Publishing. Please see last page for ordering information or to visit our website. Thank you.

More Multicultural Books

Parents' Choice Gold Award
American Bookseller Pick of the Lists
THE KIDS' MULTICULTURAL ART BOOK
Art & Craft Experiences from Around the World
by Alexandra M. Terzian
$12.95, 128 pages

Parents' Choice Approved
Benjamin Franklin Best Multicultural Book Award
THE KIDS' MULTICULTURAL COOKBOOK
Food & Fun Around the World
by Deanna F. Cook
$12.95, 128 pages

HANDS AROUND THE WORLD
365 Creative Ways to Build Cultural Awareness & Global Respect
by Susan Milord
$12.95, 128 pages

AROUND-THE-WORLD ART & ACTIVITIES
Visiting the 7 Continents Through Craft Fun
by Judy Press
$12.95, 128 pages

American Bookseller Pick of the Lists
¡MEXICO!
40 Activities to Experience Mexico Past and Present
by Susan Milord
$12.95, 128 pages

Parents' Choice Approved
Benjamin Franklin Best Multicultural Book Award
TALES OF THE SHIMMERING SKY
Ten Global Folktales with Activities
by Susan Milord
$12.95, 128 pages

Storytelling World Honor Award
Tales Alive!
BIRD TALES from Near and Far
by Susan Milord
$12.95, 96 pages

Parents' Choice Honor Award
Benjamin Franklin Best Juvenile Fiction Award
TALES ALIVE!
Ten Multicultural Folktales with Activities
by Susan Milord
$12.95, 128 pages

WHO INVENTED MATH (and why?)
Around-the-World Activities to Explore the Mystery
by Ann McCallum
2-color, $14.95, 128 pages

Children's Book Council Notable Social Studies Trade Book
WHO *REALLY* DISCOVERED AMERICA?
Unraveling the Mystery & Solving the Puzzle
by Avery Hart
$10.95, 128 pages

Williamson's *Kids Can!*® Books

Kids Can!® books for ages 7 to 14 are 128 to 176 pages, fully illustrated, trade paper, 11 x 8 ½, $12.95 US/$19.95 CAN.

Parents' Choice Recommended
ForeWord Magazine Book of the Year Finalist
PAPER-FOLDING FUN!
50 Awesome Crafts to Weave, Twist & Curl
by Ginger Johnson

Parents' Choice Recommended
The Kids' Guide to
MAKING SCRAPBOOKS & PHOTO ALBUMS!
How to Collect, Design, Assemble, Decorate
by Laura Check

Parents' Choice Recommended
Orbus Pictus Award for Outstanding Nonfiction
KIDS' ART WORKS!
Creating with Color, Design, Texture & More
by Sandi Henry

Teachers' Choice Award
Dr. Toy Best Vacation Product
CUT-PAPER PLAY!
Dazzling Creations from Construction Paper
by Sandi Henry